I read several pages and it helped me remember. To read the refferanced Bible verses - look at a regular Bible.

Especially for

Lily

from

Great Grandma Sondra (McFalls) Keith

Date

Christmas 2022

From a great
Preason me ♡

Lilly ♡

The
PRAYER
MAP®

DEVOTIONAL

for
TEEN GIRLS

JANICE THOMPSON

The PRAYER MAP®

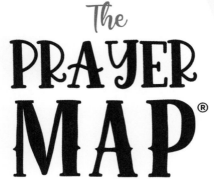

DEVOTIONAL

for

TEEN GIRLS

28 Weeks of
Inspiring Readings
∻ **PLUS** ∻
Weekly Guided
Prayer Maps

BARBOUR
PUBLISHING

Print ISBN 978-1-63609-160-0

Published by Barbour Publishing, Inc., 1810 Barbour Drive, Uhrichsville, Ohio 44683, www.barbourbooks.com

Our mission is to inspire the world with the life-changing message of the Bible.

Printed in China.

INTRODUCTION

Never stop praying.
1 THESSALONIANS 5:17 NLT

This devotional was created with you—yes, *you!*—in mind. In your heart of hearts, you want to know God more, to spend more time with Him. But life is super busy and the distractions are everywhere. School, sports, friends, church. . .you're always on the go. Sometimes you wonder if things will ever slow down long enough to figure out who God really is or how to talk to Him.

Sure, you want to be a girl who prays. Everyone says you should pray more, and you know it's true. But going to God first—instead of your friends or someone in your family? . . . Sometimes you just forget because of all the chaos swirling around you. You're not ignoring Him on purpose. You just forget.

Over the next several weeks you're going to embark on a prayer journey, one that will remind you that God is never too busy for you. He wants you to s-l-o-w down long enough to get to know Him, *really* get to know Him. For only when you truly know Him will you crave His company. (Hey, you know it's true! Did you want to spend hours hanging out with your best friend before you got to know her? Probably not!)

You can learn to go deeper with God—to share your heart in good times and bad. It's a learning process, but you can do it, girl.

Ready, set. . .pray!

Date:

DEAR GOD, *i dont want a dad Pleaje*

I'm thankful for... *My grand Parents*

My worries...

People I am praying for...

Here's what's going on in my life. . . ..
....
....
....
....

MY NEEDS. . .

....
....
....
....
....
....
....
....
....
....
....
....
....
....
....

Other stuff I need to share
with You, God. . .

....
....
....
....
....
....
....
....

AMEN.
Thank You, Father,
for hearing my prayers.

WEEK 1
Hey, Can We Talk?

"I tell you, you can pray for anything, and if
you believe that you've received it, it will be yours."
MARK 11:24 NLT

Have you ever had one of those days when you just needed someone to talk to? Maybe you texted your best friend but she was too busy to chat. Or you tried to connect with your mom but she was in the middle of fixing dinner or taking your kid brother to soccer practice.

It's not always easy to find a listening ear, but when you do, it feels really good. Whew! You can finally share all of that stuff that's been driving you nuts, the icky stuff you've been bottling up inside.

God wants you to know that He's always there, ready to listen, even when no one else is. Every day He says, "Come sit by Me and talk awhile, girl! Tell Me *all* the things. The good, the bad, and the ugly. I can take it, I promise."

You've been wondering how to get to know Him more? You've been feeling a little guilty over the "I don't pray enough" thing? It's really not that complicated.

Spill it—*all* of it. That's what He wants.

I'm so glad I can talk to You about anything and everything, Lord!
Thank You for always being there for me, no matter what! Amen.

Let's Talk about the Easy Stuff

I will say to the Lord, "You are my safe and
strong place, my God, in Whom I trust."
PSALM 91:2 NLV

Some things are easy and fun to talk about. Example: all of the cool, exciting things that are happening in your life—that choir solo you just nabbed. The news about your dad's raise. The moment you found out you made the National Honor Society.

When you're going through a wonderful, easy season filled with unexpected blessings and joys, it's easy to share your enthusiasm with others. In fact, you can hardly wait to tell them so they can celebrate with you!

Did you know this is the most tempting time to forget to spend time with God? It's true! Sometimes you run to Him when the world is falling apart but forget to include Him when everything's amazing.

He loves it when you remember to say, "Hey, God...this amazing life You've given me? I'm pretty grateful for it! I wouldn't have any of this, if not for You!"

I hope I never forget to talk to You when things are going well, Lord!
You're the One who makes it all happen, after all. Amen.

Let's Talk about the Hard Stuff

Don't worry about anything; instead, pray about everything.
Tell God what you need, and thank him for all he has done.
PHILIPPIANS 4:6 NLT

Some things are not so easy to talk about. They're just not. They're too deep, too muddy, too complicated. You keep them tucked deep in your heart and wish you could somehow release them, but figuring out how? Not easy.

If you're like most other girls, you wish you had a confidante, someone who could be trusted with the real (deep, secret) issues you're going through. Finding someone like that? Not always easy. Girls are not always that great at secrets.

God wants you to know that you can come to Him with the hard things. Even the gross, embarrassing things that you're ashamed of. If you ask, "God, can we talk about the hard stuff?" His answer will always be "Yes."

God won't turn you away. He won't stop loving you. In fact, His love will wash away the pain of anything negative you might be going through (even things you caused with your own actions).

Run to Him with the hard stuff, girl. It's time to get that off your chest, once and for all.

Okay, Lord. . .let's do this. I'm ready to talk about the hard stuff. Amen.

Let's Talk about the Other Stuff

*And the Holy Spirit helps us in our weakness. For example,
we don't know what God wants us to pray for. But the Holy Spirit
prays for us with groanings that cannot be expressed in words.*

ROMANS 8:26 NLT

Being a girl? Not always easy. All that monthly stuff? It can be a real pain. Cramps. Pain. Bloating. Feeling weird? Yeah, you're not a fan, but what can you do?

And even when you're not dealing with all that, other things about being female can get on your nerves too! Putting up with the other girls, for instance. They can be difficult to deal with sometimes. Factor in siblings who don't get along, cute boys who don't seem to notice you exist, and life can get pretty complicated.

It's not always easy to know who you can talk to about the awkward stuff. But God is right there, arms extended, saying, "You know you can bring that to Me today, right? You can!"

The really cool thing about God: nothing is awkward with Him. Like. . . *nothing*. Think of the most embarrassing thing you might have to say to a friend or loved one and then imagine saying it to God. He won't be shocked at all. In fact, He will be really, really glad you trusted Him with that information.

So, what's keeping you? You can talk to Him about all the things, girl!

Hey, God. . .do You have a little while to chat about some tough stuff?

Let's Talk about the People Stuff

For by the grace given to me I say to everyone among you not to think of himself more highly than he ought to think, but to think with sober judgment, each according to the measure of faith that God has assigned.
ROMANS 12:3 ESV

Have you ever listened to the birds singing outside your window? Different birds make different noises. Buzzards make a terrible "cawing" sound, but mourning doves? . . . They make lovely cooing noises. Very soothing—comforting, even.

Maybe you have some friends who are like those birds. Some are difficult to listen to and others are pleasant and good, easy on the ears. The ones who gossip and complain can be tough to deal with, for sure. But the ones who have your back? Priceless!

God wants you to know that you can talk to Him about all of your friends— the ones who are difficult to be around and the ones who are easy to spend time with. And He wants you to be the easy sort of friend that other people love to listen to.

Be a mourning dove in a world filled with buzzards.

Lord, I don't always like to hear from certain people. If I'm being honest, they annoy me! Teach me how to love them, please. Amen.

Let's Talk about the Hidden Stuff

*"Call to Me, and I will answer you. And I will show you
great and wonderful things which you do not know."*
JEREMIAH 33:3 NLV

You know it's true: there are a few things you've done, or maybe things you're thinking about doing, that aren't so great. Most girls have at least a few secret sins they've tucked away, things they're not confessing to anyone—not their mom, not their BFF, not even that sister coming home from college, the one who knows so much about the world.

There are things you're so embarrassed about, so ashamed of, and you can't stand the way you feel when you remember. In fact, you're wishing you could get the gross feelings to go away forever.

Here's some good news for you today! Jesus wants to shine His light on those hidden, secret things. . .not so that He can hurt you or embarrass you or make you feel bad, but so that you can be forgiven and walk in total freedom.

What have you tucked away, girl? What's eating at your conscience? Trust Him with the hidden things, no matter how deep you have to dig to reveal them.

*This isn't going to be easy, Lord, but I've got some
secrets I need to talk to You about. . . .*

Date

DEAR GOD,

I'm thankful for. . .

My worries. . .

People I am praying for. . .

Here's what's going on in my life. . .

MY NEEDS. . .

Other stuff I need to share
with You, God. . .

AMEN.
Thank You, Father,
for hearing my prayers.

WEEK 2

People: They're Driving Me Crazy

*I want [people] everywhere to pray. They should lift up holy
hands as they pray. They should not be angry or argue.*

1 TIMOTHY 2:8 NLV

Not everyone is easy to get along with. In fact, some people are ridiculously difficult in every way. They drive you nuts. That girl in your science class, the one who's always giving you a hard time? Yeah, her. And that boy on the bus who won't stop annoying you? Yep, another one. Could he just move to another school? Please. . . ?

Sometimes it's even hard to get along with people in your own family. You find yourself asking, "Why, Lord? Why did You pick this family for me? Are You sure You got it right?"

Here's a simple truth: God created His kids to have different personalities, and sometimes they clash. But He loves all of you the same and wants you to get along the best you can. So don't give up, even on the awkward relationships. Sometimes they turn out to be the very best ones. And that boy on the bus. . . ? Maybe he just needs a friend.

*Help me to be a friend to everyone, Lord,
even the ones who drive me crazy. Amen.*

Family: The Good, the Bad, and the Ugly

*"By this everyone will know that you are
my disciples, if you love one another."*
JOHN 13:35 NIV

Family: the good, the bad, and the ugly. Let's get real: the ugly sometimes outweighs the pretty. The people who are the hardest to live with are often the ones that you actually physically live with. Your parents, your siblings, even those other relatives that you see frequently. . .they can make life tough.

If it's true that absence makes the heart grow fonder, then being with people around the clock sometimes causes struggles. So, how do you deal with the day-in-and-day-out turmoil of living with people who are not always easy to live with?

Patience. Learning to love the way God loves. Deep breaths. Acting instead of reacting. There are all sorts of strategies the Lord can show you to make those relationships better. He will, you know. He really, truly wants you to live at peace in your own home.

*Lord, I live with some tough-to-get-along-with people!
Help me learn to respond as You would respond, I pray. Amen.*

Friends: A Roller-Coaster Ride Every Day

A man who has friends must be a friend,
but there is a friend who stays nearer than a brother.
PROVERBS 18:24 NLV

People! They can be like a roller-coaster ride every day, even your closest friends. Your BFF? She's up, she's down, she's all around. You never know how she'll act on any given day. And your best guy friend goes up and down like a yo-yo too! Some days he's in a great mood and other days, like the time when he got into a fight with his dad, he can be pretty hard to deal with.

Here's the truth, girl: sometimes you're a little hard to live with too. And sometimes your emotions go up and down like everyone else's. It's just part of life.

So, how do you survive the roller coaster? Don't overreact. Don't make things bigger than they already are. You can pray through the valleys and celebrate the victories as they come.

Lord, my friends are worth it! Thanks for
surrounding me with great people. Amen.

The Ones I Love Most

"And as for me, far be it from me that I should sin against the Lord by not praying for you. But I will teach you the good and the right way."
1 SAMUEL 12:23 NLV

You're crazy about them. . . . The little kids in that class you teach at church. That elderly woman who lives on your street. Your aunt, who spoils you so much. Your mom. Your BFF. You love them with a passion and would do anything for them. But even they aren't perfect. You've had a few hiccups in your relationships—things that got uncomfortable. Mostly, though, things with your inner circle are good and you want to keep them that way.

That's why God has called you to pray for those people! He strategically placed you in a position to pray for that aunt, that elderly woman, and those little children. Did you ever consider the fact that perhaps you're the only one lifting up their names in prayer? (That's a sobering thought, isn't it? No pressure!)

God has called you to this circle for a reason. Keep on praying and believing for those you love. They're doing the same for you.

I'll keep praying for the people in
my circle, Lord! I won't give up. Amen.

Those Mean Girls, Though. . .

Respect and give thanks for those who try to bring bad to you.
Pray for those who make it very hard for you. Whoever hits you
on one side of the face, turn so he can hit the other side also.
Whoever takes your coat, give him your shirt also.
LUKE 6:28–29 NLV

It's not always easy to pray for the mean ones, is it? Those girls who go out of their way to make your life miserable. Is it really possible that God wants you to pray for them and care about their well-being too?

Today's scripture makes it clear: praying for the ones who try to "bring bad to you" is a command. But how? And why? Why would God command such a thing? Doesn't He see how awful they are?

Here's the truth—He's in the restoration business. The Creator of the universe wants to convince you that He's still creating new things—in hearts, lives, and relationships. So don't give up, even with the situations (and people) that feel impossible. He's a God of the impossible, after all!

Lord, I'll pray for mean girls, but it's going to be tough. Help me
with the people who are making my life miserable, please. Amen.

People I Should Care More About

*As for other matters, brothers and sisters, pray for us
that the message of the Lord may spread rapidly
and be honored, just as it was with you.*
2 THESSALONIANS 3:1 NIV

You hardly ever think about them until you see a story on social media or the news—those people in other countries who are being persecuted for their faith. . . . Those who are being put to death for believing in God, or those who are dying of starvation. It's easier *not* to think about them, isn't it?

Today God wants to remind you that He thinks about them day and night and hopes you'll begin to devote some time to them when you pray. Maybe you could choose a specific country to pray for. Or maybe you could alternate from place to place around the globe as the year goes on. Regardless of how you choose to do it, don't forget those on other continents and in other countries who need someone to intervene for them.

Lord, today I come to You with the people of _____ on my mind.

Date: 5, 1 0 23

DEAR GOD, ~~~~~~~~~~~~~~~~

I'm thankful for. . .

My worries. . .

People I am praying for. . .

Here's what's going on in my life. . .

MY NEEDS. . .

Other stuff I need to share with You, God. . .

AMEN.
Thank You, Father,
for hearing my prayers.

WEEK 3
I'm So Thankful!

Every good and perfect gift is from above, coming down from the Father of the heavenly lights, who does not change like shifting shadows.
JAMES 1:17 NIV

God is the giver of all good things. Today's verse says that every good and perfect gift comes from Him. Every. Single. One. If your life is filled with "good things," then you know who's behind them all! The food on your table? The cute clothes you're wearing? Those new shoes? That house you live in? Yep, it's all because of Him. He cares about every single detail of your life and makes sure to provide all you need and more. He also thought of the fun things—like mountain peaks and ocean waves and puppy dog tails. That's the kind of God He is.

He loves it when your thankful heart spills over and joy bubbles to the surface. That goofy grin on your face? He put it there. That dance move you feel like doing? He put that there too. Those people you want to share the news with? He's guided them to you so that you could share.

Most of all, He loves it when you look up and say, "Hey, God! This is all because of You! If You hadn't blessed me, if You hadn't loved me so much, so many amazing things wouldn't be happening in my life."

I'm so thankful for all the blessings, Lord!

An Attitude of Gratitude

"He that is faithful with little things is faithful with big things also.
He that is not honest with little things is not honest with big things."
LUKE 16:10 NLV

Part of having a great prayer life is recognizing that God created you to have an attitude of gratitude. Sure, it's easy to take things for granted. You forget to thank your parents for working so hard to provide for you. You don't always thank that clerk at the grocery store who waits on you or the guy who opens the door for you to walk through. But if you remember to be grateful for the little things, how much more grateful will you be when God blesses you with big things?

Here's a fun tidbit: God wants you to be grateful for. . .you. That body? Yeah, there are things about it you wish you could change, but aren't you grateful for all of the things that miraculous body can do? You have eyes that see, ears that hear, a heart that beats in steady rhythm, and fingers that curl around objects to pick them up. You have feet that get you from place to place and a perfectly formed mouth to eat and speak.

Every single detail was (and is) a gift from God. When you pause to really think about all the miracles He performed just while creating you, it's mind-boggling!

Today, I'm grateful for me, Lord!

He's Working It Out!

Trust in the LORD with all your heart,
and do not lean on your own understanding.
PROVERBS 3:5 ESV

"God is working it out." Maybe you've heard those words and you scratched your head. If God is working things out, why doesn't He just go ahead and fix them right now and get it over with? And why should He have to work? He's God, after all! He could just point His finger and take care of the problem in an instant!

He could, but sometimes He's really working out the things going on inside of you. Those emotions? Those attitudes you need to adjust? Those behaviors that need to change? Maybe your prayers are being answered instantly because God is on the move in other ways that you cannot see, working behind the scenes inside of you, girl. (Just keeping it real.)

Don't stop praying. Don't get impatient when He doesn't work things out instantly. Trust that He's got a bigger plan than what you can see with your own two eyes, and allow Him to work it out in His own way.

I trust that You're working behind the scenes, even now, Lord! Amen.

It's the Little Things

Every good and perfect gift is from above, coming down from the Father of the heavenly lights, who does not change like shifting shadows.
JAMES 1:17 NIV

Some days are so ridiculous that it's hard to find anything good in them. Maybe you've had a terrible day at school. You've failed a test or a teacher has falsely accused you of cheating. Then a thousand other little things go wrong as the day progresses. Ugh!

When you get home, your mom is mad because you forgot to clean your room before leaving for school. Or maybe your kid brother breaks your phone. Could this day possibly get any worse? Really. . . ?

Then, just about the time you're ready to give up altogether, something wonderful happens. You get an email from a teacher letting you know you've been hand-picked for the lead role in the school play.

In that moment, everything turns around! Sometimes the little things turn out to be the big things!

Thanks for the little things, Lord! They're really the big things! Amen.

Thankful for Nature

*Praise Him, sun and moon! Praise Him, all you shining stars! Praise Him,
you highest heavens, and you waters above the heavens! Let them
praise the name of the Lord! For He spoke and they came into being.*
PSALM 148:3–5 NLV

If you're ever struggling to pray, step outside. Take a walk. Go to a nearby
park or look up at the sky or the trees. When you're gazing at those fluffy
white clouds, it's easy to see that God is bigger than your situation. When you
stare up at the magnificent height of those trees, it's easy to picture that the
One who created them is big enough to handle what you're going through.

All of nature, all of creation, points to Him. He made it all for your enjoy-
ment, but He also created everything as proof that He is bigger, He is wiser,
and He is sovereign. His ways are higher. Doesn't it give you hope to know
that the One who created everything loves you more than all of it? He does,
you know! So trust Him with the things on your heart today. He's big enough
to handle them and will do so out of deep love for you.

*Lord, I see Your hand at work in nature.
Everything points to You! Amen.*

Thankful for Your Help

Dear friends, you must become strong in your most holy faith.
Let the Holy Spirit lead you as you pray.
JUDE 1:20 NLV

Don't you love the helpers? They don't need to take credit. They're usually working behind the scenes making sure everything goes smoothly for others, with no thought for their own comfort or desires.

The girl who's decorating for her best friend's party. The guy who's serving meals to the homeless. That lady at church who always smiles and greets you when you walk in on Sunday morning. Those are the worker bees. They are the helpers. They make sure the work gets done, and they don't even need a pat on the back (though it's nice to give them one).

God wants you to know that He's working behind the scenes too. Even now, in this very moment, He's hard at work putting puzzle pieces together so that your situation will turn out just the way He has planned. Never doubt that your greatest helper is working on your behalf.

Lord, thank You for the helpers! (I want to be one too!)
Most of all, thanks for being my very best help
in times of trouble. I'm so grateful. Amen.

Date

DEAR GOD, _____
_____
_____
_____

I'm thankful for. . . _____
_____
_____
_____
_____
_____
_____
_____

My worries. . . _____
_____
_____
_____
_____
_____

People I am praying for. . . _____
_____
_____
_____
_____
_____

Here's what's going on in my life. . .

MY NEEDS. . .

Other stuff I need to share with You, God. . .

AMEN.
Thank You, Father,
for hearing my prayers.

WEEK 4

I Come Boldly

*Let us go with complete trust to the throne of God.
We will receive His loving-kindness and have His
loving-favor to help us whenever we need it.*
HEBREWS 4:16 NLV

Have you ever been nervous to meet someone? Imagine you had to meet the president of the United States or the queen of England. Your knees would be knocking. Your hands would be shaking. Now imagine you were walking into heaven for the first time ready to see Jesus face-to-face. No doubt you would be overwhelmed!

Here's a really cool fact about God: the Bible says that you can come boldly to Him. You don't have to be afraid. You can walk right up to His throne without an appointment. Without any fear. Without your hands trembling or knees knocking. And you can lay your requests at His feet and fully expect that He not only hears them but will respond.

Bold faith, girl! That's what God wants to give you. So ask for His courage today and watch in amazement as He pours it out supernaturally.

*Thanks for making me bold, Lord! I need
Your supernatural courage today. Amen.*

Bold Faith

You must have faith as you ask Him. You must not doubt.
Anyone who doubts is like a wave which is pushed around
by the sea. Such a man will get nothing from the Lord.
JAMES 1:6–7 NLV

Have you ever had to ask someone a favor? Maybe you needed to borrow your sister's favorite jeans or your mom's car. Or maybe you needed to ask for something really big, like a new laptop or phone. It's one thing to ask for something when you're scared, but it's another thing to ask with boldness.

That's how God wants you to approach Him—boldly, with wild, crazy faith! He wants you to live in confidence, so ask courageously, girl. Ask, expecting that He hears you and that He loves you and wants His best for you.

Whether you're asking for help with that science test or for healing for your grandmother who's going through cancer treatment, don't ever be afraid to boldly approach your Creator. He wants to increase your faith, even now.

Lord, I want to have bold faith. I want to believe for miracles.
S-t-r-e-t-c-h my faith, please! Make me courageous in my prayers. Amen.

Bold Actions

Be on your guard; stand firm in the faith;
be courageous; be strong.
1 CORINTHIANS 16:13 NIV

Have you ever met people who seem braver than others? They speak their minds without worrying what others will think. Or maybe they stand up on the stage and sing a solo without stage fright. Nothing seems to scare them, even the *really big things*, like standing up to bullies or tackling a big problem.

Maybe you're not like that. Maybe your knees knock or your voice quivers when you have to get up in front of a group. Perhaps you have a hard time speaking your true opinions because you worry too much about what other people think of you. Maybe you wonder if you'll ever have that kind of courage.

Here's a little secret: God wants you to be bold in your actions. That means He doesn't want you to second-guess everything or to question every little move you make. When you're prayed up and ready, you can step out in faith. So straighten that spine! Move with courage toward the task ahead, girl!

I can do this, Lord. . .with Your help! Amen.

Bold Requests

*We will receive from Him whatever we
ask if we obey Him and do what He wants.*
1 JOHN 3:22 NLV

Have you ever been scared to ask your parents for something? Maybe you wanted a new outfit but it was a little on the pricey side. Or maybe you were hoping for something even bigger, like a new phone or laptop.

It's not always easy to ask for the things you want, but when you come into God's presence, when you're ready to spend time in prayer with Him, He wants you to come to Him boldly with your request. Of course, He also wants your obedience, so you can't just ask for anything you want if you're living in a way that contradicts His Word. But when your life is lined up with the Bible and you are spending time with Him, God loves to hear those requests, big or small.

So make your requests known, girl. Don't be afraid to share your heart. Your heavenly Father already knows what you're thinking anyway.

*Lord, I'm coming boldly today, ready to make
my requests known. Thanks for listening! Amen.*

Bold Witness

*"But you will receive power when the Holy Spirit comes on you;
and you will be my witnesses in Jerusalem, and in all
Judea and Samaria, and to the ends of the earth."*

ACTS 1:8 NIV

Did you know that the Bible says that all Christians should be witnessing to others? Oh, I know. . .you're hoping it will be someone else. Anyone but you. It's hard to talk to people about your faith. Sometimes they reject you or make fun of you because of your beliefs. You'd prefer to just keep them to yourself.

But think about it this way: If every believer refused to speak up, then how would the message ever get out? How would people ever know about the love of God? How would they hear the salvation message?

They wouldn't. If people cowered in fear, no one would ever come to Christ. And that, of course, is the opposite of what God wants to see happen. He longs for His kids to proclaim Him far and wide—boldly, loudly, and with great faith that people's lives will change. What an impact you can have if you'll just speak up!

*Lord, I get it. I'm supposed to be a bold witness
for You. Help me have the courage I need! Amen.*

A Bold Way to Start My Day

In the morning before the sun was up, Jesus went to a
place where He could be alone. He prayed there.

MARK 1:35 NLV

How do you kick off your day? When you first roll out of bed in the morning, what's your routine? Maybe you check your phone. Or (like most people) maybe you head to the bathroom. You prep yourself for school—brushing your teeth, showering, dressing, and so on. There are a ton of things that need to be done in a short period of time.

But one very important thing that people often overlook in the morning is prayer and Bible reading. If you will start your day in the Word, you'll be surprised at how much better things will go. For one thing, you'll have a ready answer on your lips when things go wrong. Those scriptures you just read will be on your mind. And your faith will be activated after kicking off the day in prayer. You can also suit up in your spiritual armor, so you're truly prepared for anything the enemy might throw your way.

Yep, starting off right is the way to go. So let's get going!

Lord, I come to You this morning, ready to get my day
off to a great start. Thanks for meeting me here!

Date:

DEAR GOD, ...
....
....
....

I'm thankful for. . . ..
....
....
....
....
....
....
....
....

My worries. . . ..
....
....
....
....
....
....

People I am praying for. . . ..
....
....
....
....
....

Here's what's going on in my life. . .

MY NEEDS. . .

Other stuff I need to share with You, God. . .

AMEN.
Thank You, Father,
for hearing my prayers.

WEEK 5

The Secret Place: Hide Me Away

"But when you pray, go away by yourself, shut the door behind you, and pray to your Father in private. Then your Father, who sees everything, will reward you."
MATTHEW 6:6 NLT

If you've ever been in a library, you know what it's like to be surrounded by books of every kind—history books, novels, comedies, political books, suspense stories, memoirs. . . Libraries have every conceivable kind of book on their shelves.

Now think about your heart. It's a lot like that library. You've got memories that are good, bad, funny, and sweet. You've got deep wounds and injuries that you keep hidden away on the top shelf so no one can touch them.

God sees the library inside your heart, and He wants to dust off every book so you can be healthy and strong and filled with His presence. And guess what? That story He's writing in your life? It's only just beginning. He wants to share many more pages, so don't give up. Allow Him into the secret places of your heart so true healing can come.

Lord, what's my story going to look like?
What chapter is coming next?

No One Else Is Listening, Lord!

*He who lives in the safe place of the Most High will be in the
shadow of the All-powerful. I will say to the Lord, "You are
my safe and strong place, my God, in Whom I trust."*

PSALM 91:1–2 NLV

Have you ever thought about what life must've been like before all the modern technology we take for granted today? No cell phones. No computers. No GPS. People stayed in touch by writing letters or visiting in person.

Even an in-person visit took a lot of effort back then, because travel was slow. No airplanes! People road-tripped by wagon train or railroad. (Can you even imagine not being able to hop in a car and get from point A to point B quickly?)

But staying in touch with Jesus is a lot less complicated than dropping in on your long-lost relatives back in the olden days. You don't even have to punch in His number on your phone. He's always nearby. All you have to do is speak His name and He's listening. And the best news of all? The call is totally free. He won't be sending you a bill for the time spent with you!

Thanks, Lord, for always being nearby. No long-distance travel for me!

Can We Talk about Something Awkward?

*"Then you will call upon Me and come and
pray to Me, and I will listen to you."*
JEREMIAH 29:12 NLV

It's awkward. It's uncomfortable. You don't want to talk about it. . .with anyone. But part of you wishes you *could* talk about it. You've got questions and concerns. You're confused and fretting. If only you knew someone trustworthy. You might just take a chance and spill your guts, ask the hard questions.

Thankfully, there is someone. He's right there, ready to hear all you have to say. He won't pressure you to dive right in either. But you could if you wanted to. Nothing—truly, nothing—shocks Him.

Today is the perfect day to open up to Jesus. Once you get this conversation behind you, everything will change. But it starts with trusting Him enough to say, "Lord, can we talk about something awkward?" His answer is—and always will be—"Yes."

*Lord, I'm coming to You today with something difficult to talk about.
I don't really know how to say it, but I want to share something
totally awkward with You. Thanks for letting me, Lord. Amen.*

Sometimes I Feel Weak

Look to the Lord and ask for His strength.
Look to Him all the time.
1 CHRONICLES 16:11 NLV

If you're like most girls, you like to pretend things are perfect even when they're not. In fact, you've become so skilled at it that people don't even notice you're having an "off" day.

But let's admit it—some days you're just not feeling it. Sometimes you're so exhausted, so run-down, that you're not even sure you can get out of bed, let alone get dressed and go to school and face all the challenges ahead of you. (Ugh! Ever have a day like that?)

On those days especially, you need to look to Jesus. He can give you His supernatural strength in those beyond-ridiculous moments. It's amazing, really. He will not only wake you up and zap you with heavenly energy but will also give you a new excitement about the day ahead. So trust Him. Even on the weak days.

Lord, I'll admit it. I'm not feeling it today. I'm weak.
Can You zap me with Your strength, please? Amen.

Sometimes I Get a Little Selfish

Or if you do ask, you do not receive because your reasons for asking are wrong. You want these things only to please yourselves.

JAMES 4:3 NLV

If someone asked the question, "Are you selfish?" how would you respond? Do you consider yourself to be self-centered? Most people don't see their own selfishness unless someone else points it out to them. In fact, most people would say, "I'm the opposite of selfish. I'm always doing everything for everyone."

Are you, though? Maybe it's time for a reality check. If you added up the minutes you spend each day pouring yourself into others, how many minutes would that come to? Perhaps not as many as you claim!

You might also check your motivation. Are you doing those things before you are asked? Do you automatically think of how you can serve and help others without anyone asking you first? God wants to give you a servant's heart. (No, really.) He wants you to be motivated to put others before yourself. It's not easy, but He can show you how.

I'm really going to need Your help with this one, Lord. Amen.

Sometimes I Get a Little Lazy

The path of the lazy man is grown over with thorns,
but the path of the faithful is a good road.
PROVERBS 15:19 NLV

Don't you love those lazy days? Sunday afternoons. Saturday mornings. Hanging out in your pj's. Chilling. Watching TV. A quiet conversation with a friend. These are the days you long for.

Unfortunately, not all lazy days are meant to be lazy. There are days when you really should be doing something productive, but you just aren't feeling it. So you make excuses. You've got a headache. You don't feel well. You're tired. And all the things that needed to get done? Well, you've pushed them off till tomorrow. Only, tomorrow's hours are already slotted for something else.

If you want to get this situation turned around and increase your energy level and become productive, there's an easy solution: give your days to God. Tell Him every morning that your hours are really His. Then listen to His still, small voice so He can tell you whether to rest, play, or work.

I trust You with all my days, Lord. I want to be found faithful. Amen.

Date:

DEAR GOD, ...
....
....
....

I'm thankful for. . . ..
....
....
....
....
....
....
....
....

My worries. . . ..
....
....
....
....
....

People I am praying for. . . ..
....
....
....
....
....

Here's what's going on in my life. . .

MY NEEDS. . .

Other stuff I need to share
with You, God. . .

AMEN.
Thank You, Father,
for hearing my prayers.

WEEK 6

Can We Talk about This Body You Gave Me?

"Before I formed you in the womb I knew you, before you were born I set you apart; I appointed you as a prophet to the nations."
JEREMIAH 1:5 NIV

You don't mean to complain, but certain things about your body bug you. And you wish you could change them. You notice every bump, every mole or freckle. And you're not keen on any of it. Why did God make you so flawed, so different from everyone else?

Sure, He created you in His image and you're grateful, but you're also a little curious about what He must look like if He looks like all the people He created. Some parts of you can't be changed—your skin color, freckles, eyes, and so on. Other things you've already tried to change—your hair color, your too-skinny legs, even your waist size.

But remember this. . .*before* you were ever formed in your mother's womb, God knew you. And guess what? He loved you, even then. He knew exactly how you would turn out, and He wasn't one bit disappointed!

I'd like to spend some time talking to You about how—
and why—You created me the way You did, Lord.
I'm not complaining. Honest. I'm just curious! Amen.

Things I'm Okay With

I praise you, for I am fearfully and wonderfully made.
Wonderful are your works; my soul knows it very well.
PSALM 139:14 ESV

If you're like most girls, you look in the mirror and find things to complain about. But—admit it!—there are things about your appearance you like too. (Hey, it's not all bad, is it?)

So what's your favorite part of you? Your nose? Your hair? Your curves? Before you say, "I can't think of one thing," take the time to really think it through. Do you have cute fingernails? Sandal-worthy feet? The perfect ears? A winning smile? A vibrant personality?

Surely you can celebrate something when you stare at that reflection in the mirror. And remember, you're created in God's image, and He's celebrating when He looks at you. So don't forget to give yourself a rousing "Ta-da!" next time you look in the mirror. You are fearfully and wonderfully made, after all. And God doesn't make mistakes—so join in the celebration.

Lord, there really are certain parts of me that I'm okay with.
Here are just a few, Lord. . .(fill in the blank). Amen!

The Parts of Me That Are Changing

For everything there is a season,
and a time for every matter under heaven.
ECCLESIASTES 3:1 ESV

Don't you love to watch butterflies flitting across the sky? They move with such ease, as if floating on the wind. Their lives look carefree and painless, but they're really not! Butterflies go through an amazing transformation, and they have to trust the Creator at every stage, from chrysalis to flight.

You've gone through a lot of transformations too. In fact, you're probably going through a few now—physically, emotionally, even spiritually. You're a beautiful butterfly, girl, emerging from the cocoon and floating across the sky. Instead of arguing with God about your stage of transformation, begin to thank Him for growing you into an amazing young woman, fully loved by Him at every single phase.

You're beautiful—right here, right now. Never doubt it for even a second!

Thank You for the reminder that You're still working in my body,
heart, and mind, Lord. I'm changing. . .and that's okay!

My Attitude Might Need Adjusting!

Have this mind among yourselves,
which is yours in Christ Jesus.
PHILIPPIANS 2:5 ESV

Many years ago—back in the 1970s and '80s—there was a fun saying in church youth groups. Whenever the kids would get too rowdy, the youth leader would holler, "Attitude check!" and the youth would respond with, "Praise the Lord!"

That might seem like a silly exercise, but it was a great reminder that when you're having a bad day or just don't feel like cooperating with the rest of humanity—the answer is always the same: *Praise the Lord!*

What's going on in your heart today? Are you irritated, frustrated, or nervous? No matter what you're feeling, you can turn it all around with a "Praise the Lord" adjustment. When you shift your complaint (or your worries) to Him, you forget about the bad because you're reminded of His greatness. He *is* great, you know, and He's bigger than whatever you're facing. So trust Him to make the necessary adjustments—in His time and His way—so that your not-so-great day can turn around.

You're greater, Lord! Check my attitude today, I pray. Amen.

All These Changes, Though!

*I appeal to you therefore, brothers, by the mercies of God,
to present your bodies as a living sacrifice, holy and
acceptable to God, which is your spiritual worship.*
ROMANS 12:1 ESV

If you're paying attention to what's going on outside your window, you'll notice that things are always changing. The garden out front looks different in the spring and summer than it does in the fall and winter. Friendships change. And appearances. Your mom looks different than she did several years ago.

Maybe you're not cool with all the changes. You don't like the fact that your face is covered in acne or that you randomly put on ten pounds.

But there's good news for you today: change is a good thing. It's growing you into the woman you will become. If you can stand steady like that tree in your yard, if you can withstand all the changes in the good times and bad, your roots will grow deep and you will be a woman of strength and power someday. So hang in there, girl!

*You're growing me into something—someone—different than
who I've been. Help me with the changes, Lord! Amen.*

What Will I Look Like Ten Years from Now?

And I am sure of this, that he who began a good work in you will bring it to completion at the day of Jesus Christ.
PHILIPPIANS 1:6 ESV

You're probably wondering what you'll look like when you get older. Will you even recognize yourself? Will your body change a lot over time, or will you still look pretty much the same? (This might be a good time to ask your mom for a picture of herself as a teen.)

You're going to change a lot over the coming years. Those changes won't happen overnight, but your body will continue to mature. Your heart will mature too. The dreams that God planted there will blossom and grow if you water them and tend to them. This will require work from you—you'll have to spend time reading the Bible, praying, and committing yourself to His call on your life.

Yes, your body will change. Your attitude might change. But one thing will never change: God will be just as crazy about you when you're older as He is right now. (And He's pretty crazy about you right now!)

I'm kind of glad I don't know what my body will look like years from now, Lord, but I trust You with the process!

Date:

DEAR GOD, ...
....
....
....

I'm thankful for. . . ..
....
....
....
....
....
....
....

My worries. . . ..
....
....
....
....
....

People I am praying for. . . ..
....
....
....
....

Here's what's going on in my life. . .

MY NEEDS. . .

Other stuff I need to share with You, God. . .

AMEN.
Thank You, Father,
for hearing my prayers.

WEEK 7

Everything Points to Him!

*"For God so loved the world, that he gave his only Son,
that whoever believes in him should not perish but have eternal life."*

JOHN 3:16 ESV

All of creation points to God. It's true! The rushing rivers, hooting owls, and majestic mountain peaks all cry out, "Look at us! We were created with the breath and the finger of God!"

Your kid sister, your best friend, even your not-so-favorite teacher. . . they're all pointing to God too. They're living, breathing humans, created in His image.

And you? Every cell, every microscopic part of your anatomy, points to Him. He took the time to craft you in such a detailed way—from numbering the hairs on your head to the splattering of freckles on your nose.

If God cared this much—to create all of this so that the world would know Him—how can you help but point to Him too! You're a reflection of your Creator, girl. Shine on, so that all can come to know Him!

*Lord, I get it. You created me to point to You.
May I do that today in the best possible way. Amen.*

The Heavens Point to Him!

*Let the heavens be glad, and let the earth rejoice; let the sea roar,
and all that fills it; let the field exult, and everything in it!
Then shall all the trees of the forest sing for joy.*

PSALM 96:11–12 ESV

Who hung the skies in place? Who scattered twinkling stars to shine at night and a vast sun to beam down on you during the daytime hours? Who divided light from darkness? Who created other planets and moons, flinging them out into space?

The heavens were specifically designed by the ultimate Creator, God. And every magnificent detail points to Him. Those shimmering stars cry out, "We're a reflection of His light!" Those fluffy clouds whisper, "He made us too!"

Today, spend some time examining the sky above you. No doubt you'll come away mesmerized by the brilliant blues, the fluffy whites, and the beautiful nighttime sky, littered with twinkling fairy lights.

He did it all for you, girl, so that you could have a little surprise glimpse of what heaven will one day be like.

*It's going to be amazing, Lord! If the skies are just a glimpse
of heaven, the real deal is going to blow me away!*

Problems Point to Him

*"The thief comes only to steal and kill and destroy.
I came that they may have life and have it abundantly."*
JOHN 10:10 ESV

God isn't the one who created your problems. Let that sink in a minute. When some people are going through a hard time, they point to heaven and say, "Why are You doing this to me, Lord?"

But God isn't the author of confusion and pain. The enemy of our souls has come to steal, kill, and destroy. So anything that brings pain or confusion is a tool he's using against you. God has come to bring abundant life.

Still, He can use your current problems to grow you. When you're faced with a challenge, let it point you straight back to God. Instead of looking to your friends or loved ones for answers, look to Jesus. He's not only got a way out of this problem; He promises to use it for His glory. In the end, life will be abundant, as long as you give Him the reins.

*Lord, I haven't always experienced "abundant life." There have
been problems. Lots of them. Today I give those problems
back to You and ask You to work them all out for good.*

People Point to You

"In the same way, let your light shine before others, that they may see your good deeds and glorify your Father in heaven."
MATTHEW 5:16 NIV

All you have to do is look around you at the people in your world to see that they are pointing to God. You might read that sentence and say, "Well, the ones who are living right are pointing to Him, but I'm not so sure about the ones who refuse to live right."

Here's the truth—you're learning from their mistakes, so (in a sense) they're still pointing you toward your Creator. After all, we do learn from the bad as well as the good.

Here's a question for you: What are people learning about God by examining *your* life? Are they seeing lots of great illustrations of faith, courage, tenacity, and hope? Or are they having to learn from your mistakes instead? Be the sort of Christian who points the way with courage and determination, one who tries to live right.

Lord, I want to point people to You—for all the right reasons. When they examine my life, may they see joy, peace, hope, and bravery, I pray. Amen.

My Desire to Learn Points to You

Let the wise hear and increase in learning,
and the one who understands obtain guidance.
PROVERBS 1:5 ESV

You're on a never-ending learning curve, which means you're always going to be discovering something new. (Hey, you thought the "schooling" stopped when you graduated from college? Not even close!)

God has so much to teach you—things you can't learn in books. But don't worry! He's a great teacher—patient and loving. And He wants to "grow" your desire to learn so that you can do marvelous things for Him. This means you're going to be in His classroom. . .forever. Yep, you read that right. *Forever.*

Today, make up your mind to be a terrific student. Let God teach you—through His Word, His people, His creation. He's got so much more for you than you dared to dream! Open your heart to the possibilities, and then see where the road takes you. (Hint: it takes you to the places He longs for you to go.)

Lord, I'm open to learning all that You have for me. Today I offer my heart, my mind, and my will to You, so that I can be the best student ever! Amen.

My Actions (Should!) Point to You

*What good is it, my brothers, if someone says he has faith
but does not have works? Can that faith save him?*
JAMES 2:14 ESV

It's your turn to wash the dishes. *Again.* Not your favorite chore. You would rather do something fun, like hang out with your friends. But have you ever thought about what would happen if no one did the dishes? All the germs from previous meals would get on any new food that you put on that plate. You would end up sick if it didn't get cleaned. Ick!

The same is true when it comes to dealing with sin in your life. If you don't deal with it, if you don't allow Christ to wash it away, then you will not thrive. God wants you to thrive, to be healthy and strong. So allow Him to put you under the faucet, girl! He's got some work to do in your heart today. He's happy to take on this task.

*Lord, I come to You, ready to admit that my actions aren't always
the best. I don't like to carry through with ordinary tasks. But You?
When it comes to cleansing my heart, You're the best!*

Date:

DEAR GOD, ...

....

....

....

I'm thankful for. . . ..

....

....

....

....

....

....

....

....

My worries. . . ..

....

....

....

....

....

....

People I am praying for. . . ..

....

....

....

....

....

Here's what's going on in my life. . .

MY NEEDS. . .

Other stuff I need to share with You, God. . .

AMEN.
Thank You, Father,
for hearing my prayers.

WEEK 8

Does Prayer Change Anything?

"But if you remain in me and my words remain in you,
you may ask for anything you want, and it will be granted!"
JOHN 15:7 NLT

You wonder if your prayers are actually working. You've poured out so many of them lately, but it's like crickets on the other end. If God is listening, He sure seems to be quiet up there. Maybe He's so busy taking care of the rest of the world that He doesn't have time for you. Or maybe there's some big problem in the Middle East that's more pressing to Him at the moment.

Here's a cool fact about God: He can handle it all. At once. And to Him, your broken heart is equally as important as a world catastrophe. It's true. He cares as much about you as He does anyone (or anything) else. So rest easy that He not only hears your prayers but He's already working behind the scenes (even when you don't sense it).

Trust Him. Your prayers are definitely making a difference, so don't stop, no matter what.

Lord, I won't give up. I'll keep praying, even when
answers seem a long time in coming. Amen.

Can You Change My Heart?

*All Scripture is breathed out by God and profitable for teaching,
for reproof, for correction, and for training in righteousness, that the
man of God may be competent, equipped for every good work.*
2 TIMOTHY 3:16–17 ESV

Are you a dog lover? Dogs can be a wonderful addition to a home, but they can also be messy, naughty, and expensive! Still, with proper training, they are worth the effort. The kind of patience that it takes to train a pup for service is exactly what it's going to take you to train your very own heart and mind.

Maybe that idea offends you. "What? Now I'm a dog?" Nope! But you can be trained in much the same way. . .by repetition. Reading your Bible every day. Praying, even when you don't feel like it. Adjusting your attitude instead of arguing. Listening instead of speaking. These are some repetitive habits that can shape you into a godly woman (and can spare you a lot of pain later on).

God can change your heart. He can also change your mind. Most of all, He can change your habits. So lean on Him today. Make a list of all the things you wish you could change. . .then offer that list to Him.

*Lord, You can change my heart. Today I give it to You and ask You
to do just that. I want to be shaped into Your image, Father. Amen.*

Can You Change My Circumstances?

*We are sure that if we ask anything that He wants us to have,
He will hear us. If we are sure He hears us when we ask,
we can be sure He will give us what we ask for.*

1 JOHN 5:14–15 NLV

You're not a fan of the circumstances you're currently in. In fact, you wish they would change. . .immediately. They're uncomfortable, irritating, and a pain in the neck—if you're being totally honest.

But sometimes circumstances don't seem to change. They just drag on from year to year. Angry people stay angry. Drunks stay drunk. Drug addicts stay addicted. And as you watch them, you begin to lose hope.

Does this mean God isn't on the job? No! He's right there, tugging on the hearts of the ones who need to change. He's also working behind the scenes on big projects, like finding a new job for your dad or fixing that broken heart your mom's been living with for so long.

God is in the "changing and fixing" business, girl. It might not be on your timetable, but He is always working, working, working to make things better.

*Lord, I trust Your timing. Please fix the broken circumstances
in my life and in the lives of those I love. Amen.*

Can You Change the People around Me?

You may see a Christian brother sinning in a way that does not lead to death. You should pray for him. God will give him life unless he has done that sin that leads to death. There is a sin that leads to death. There is no reason to pray for him if he has done that sin.

1 JOHN 5:16 NLV

You wonder if mean girls will always be mean. You're convinced that awful teacher will always be awful. And you're absolutely sure that one boy—the one who broke your heart—will go on playing the field, breaking other hearts as well. In short, you've given up on those people. You don't see them as capable of change.

Maybe they aren't. But you know who *is* capable of changing them? God. That's why it's important to keep praying, even for the seemingly impossible cases—the "she's never going to change" friends (or ex-friends, as the case may be). God loves them as much as He loves you. It's hard to imagine, but it's true. And He longs for their hearts to turn to Him as well.

So don't give up. Maybe the role you're supposed to play in all of their lives is to intercede (pray) so they can (finally!) come to know Him and see their lives radically changed.

Lord, it's hard to pray for the tough cases, but I won't give up. Please change the people around me. Amen.

Can You Change My Country?

"If My people who are called by My name put away their pride and pray, and look for My face, and turn from their sinful ways, then I will hear from heaven. I will forgive their sin, and will heal their land."

2 CHRONICLES 7:14 NLV

Rioting. Looting. People turning against people. Friends arguing about vaccines and masks. It's all a big mess, isn't it? Like the world didn't have enough trouble already! You want to make things better, but half the time you just end up in the middle of the arguments, stating your opinion.

It's time to step back and take a different approach, girl. Instead of joining the debate, become a prayer warrior. Use this tumultuous time to drop to your knees and pray—for your country, for your state, for your neighbors, and for all of those who carry so much anger.

Today's verse is very clear: God can and will hear from heaven and forgive the sins of our nation(s) but only if we do four things—put away our pride (stop arguing); pray; look for His face (instead of looking for answers from each other or the government); and turn from sinful ways. Someone has to stand in the gap. Will that someone be you?

Lord, it will be me! I'll stand in the gap—for my country, my friends, and my family. Forgive our sins and heal our land, I pray! Amen.

Can You Change This World? (Corporate Prayer)

"Again I tell you this: If two of you agree on earth about anything you pray for, it will be done for you by My Father in heaven. For where two or three are gathered together in My name, there I am with them."
MATTHEW 18:19–20 NLV

Have you ever heard the phrase "corporate prayer"? It's when two or more people come together and agree to pray about the same thing. They link arms to make a difference. There's power in numbers, for sure!

The Bible says that if two or more of you agree on earth about anything you pray for, it will be done for you in heaven. That's a powerful promise! So maybe it's time to gather the troops. Link arms. Be like a red rover team, a long invincible line that the enemy can't penetrate. Then, from a position of strength, link your prayers together for the big stuff—your sick grandmother, your parents' divorce, your father's anger problems, your neighbor's drug addiction.

Don't go it alone, girl. You were never meant to. Grab a like-minded Christian friend and get her on board. Then watch as God intervenes on your behalf.

*Thank You for the reminder that I don't
have to do this by myself, Lord! Amen.*

71

Date:

DEAR GOD, _____
_____
_____
_____

I'm thankful for. . . _____
_____
_____
_____
_____
_____
_____
_____

My worries. . . _____
_____
_____
_____
_____
_____

People I am praying for. . . _____
_____
_____
_____
_____

Here's what's going on in my life. . .

MY NEEDS. . .

Other stuff I need to share with You, God. . .

AMEN.
Thank You, Father,
for hearing my prayers.

WEEK 9

Stop to Smell the Roses

*It is in vain that you rise up early and go late to rest, eating the
bread of anxious toil; for he gives to his beloved sleep.*
PSALM 127:2 ESV

You're busy. Crazy busy. Insanely busy. You hardly have time to stop and catch your breath before you're on to the next class. Or project. Or event. Whew!

In the middle of your busyness, it's not always easy to remember to stop to smell the roses. You have bigger things to do. But God doesn't want you to forget to take care of yourself along the way. So take that bubble bath. Enjoy that quiet time with your grandmother. Have a quick visit with an old friend. And as you do, be reminded that there's more to life than a crazy busy schedule. When all is said and done it's not the busyness you will remember. It's those special God-breathed moments of beauty. The times you paused to gaze up at the twinkling night sky. The moments you picked up the phone to call an elderly grandparent. The kind note you paused to write to that stressed teacher.

Stop to smell the roses, girl. You'll be glad you did.

*Lord, thank You for the reminder that I need to pause from the craziness
to have special God-moments. I want more of those, Lord! Amen.*

I'm Slowing Down to Be with You!

*"But when you pray, go into your room and shut
the door and pray to your Father who is in secret.
And your Father who sees in secret will reward you."*
MATTHEW 6:6 ESV

Have you ever added too much salt to your food? Too much can ruin a perfectly good meal! That's kind of how it is with many things in your life: a little is good, but a lot?. . . Too much! Take time with your friends, for instance. Maybe it's best to take them in small doses. And that yummy chocolate cake you want to eat for dessert? Eat too much and you'll end up sick.

There's one thing that you can never have too much of, though. That's time with Jesus! You could spend hours a day talking to Him and your relationship would never get too salty. In fact, the more you hang out with Him, the more balanced your life becomes. So take some time out of your crazy schedule to spend a few minutes with Jesus. You'll be so glad you did. (And He'll be pretty glad too!)

*Lord, I'm sorry I've let my busyness keep me from You.
Today I come—even if it's just for a few minutes—
to spend time hanging out with You. Amen.*

I'm Slowing Down to Enjoy My Family

For this reason I bow my knees before the Father,
from whom every family in heaven and on earth is named.
EPHESIANS 3:14–15 ESV

You don't always take the time for family like you should. In fact, they are often the lowest when it comes to your priorities. You would rather make time for your friends, your peers, and your activities.

But don't leave out those family members, girl! They are the reason you're here! They need you, and you need them. So don't forget to spend time praying for them and making time for their needs, as well as your own.

There will come a day when you're grown and gone from home. You will long for these days again and will wish that you had spent more time with those family members. So take advantage of that time now. Give of yourself.

Not just to your friends, but to your family as well.

Lord, thank You for my family. I don't want to take
them for granted or neglect them! Show me how
to make the time and love them like You do. Amen.

I'm Slowing Down to Enjoy My Friends

Two are better than one, because they have good pay for their work.
For if one of them falls, the other can help him up. But it is hard
for the one who falls when there is no one to lift him up.
ECCLESIASTES 4:9–10 NLV

God has given you some remarkable friends, hasn't He? Tall, short, skinny, chubby, in every color of the rainbow. . .they're yours, and you love them!

Some will be friends for just a short time; others will be friends for years to come. One thing is for sure. . .those friends need your prayers. They are going through a lot, just like you are. So as you settle into your quiet time with Jesus, don't forget to lift their names in prayer as well. The one whose parents are going through a divorce. The one who's struggling with insecurities. The one who confided in you that she's contemplated suicide. They all need your prayers.

And don't forget to ask them to pray for you too. Iron sharpens iron. Friends stay strong when they stick together in prayer.

Lord, thank You for the reminder that I need to pray more for my friend.
I'll help her up when she falls, and I know she'll do the same for me.

I'm Slowing Down to Enjoy This Planet

By faith we understand that the universe was created by the word of God,
so that what is seen was not made out of things that are visible.
HEBREWS 11:3 ESV

What a creative God we serve! He made everything—from lizards that slither from place to place, turning green to brown in an instant, to alligators with snapping jaws, to newborn kittens curled up at their mother's side. He took His fingertip and formed mountain peaks and valleys deep. And with a word He hung the sun, moon, and stars in place. That night sky you love? It's all because of Him.

Sometimes days go by, and you're so busy that you forget to notice your surroundings. That beautiful green grass in the yard. Those flowers in the flower bed. That cool afternoon breeze. He made all of it for your viewing pleasure, so don't overlook it.

Today, take the time to s-l-o-w down and take in your surroundings. Then take another moment to thank the Creator of it all for making it just for you.

Lord, I love all the things You've created! May I never forget
that You went to great efforts to make my surroundings
so beautiful. Thank You, Father! Amen.

I'm Slowing Down for My Church

They were faithful in listening to the teaching of the missionaries.
They worshiped and prayed and ate the Lord's supper together.
ACTS 2:42 NLV

You make room for everyone else. . .your friends, loved ones, family members, and yourself. How are you doing when it comes to your church? Are you praying for your pastor and all those other hard workers? Are you committed? Do you show up—body, soul, and spirit? Are you engaged in what's happening from week to week?

God wants your relationship with your local church to be more than just a "have to" sort of thing. He wants you to want to go to church. In fact, God wants you to look forward to it with so much anticipation that you can't wait to get there!

Maybe you're struggling with this. Could be, you don't even like going . . .at all. Here's a little clue: if you will begin to pray for your church now, for people to grow stronger and for God's Spirit to be free to move in that place, you will view your together time a lot differently. Fall in love with Jesus as deeply as you can, and He will give you a love for your local church that will change everything.

Lord, show me how to pray for my church, please. Amen.

Date:

DEAR GOD, ...
....
....
....

I'm thankful for. . . ..
....
....
....
....
....
....
....

My worries. . . ..
....
....
....
....
....
....

People I am praying for. . . ..
....
....
....
....
....

Here's what's going on in my life. . .

MY NEEDS. . .

Other stuff I need to share
with You, God. . .

AMEN.
Thank You, Father,
for hearing my prayers.

WEEK 10

This Isn't What I Signed Up For!

You must keep praying. Keep watching! Be thankful always.
COLOSSIANS 4:2 NLV

Life can go crazy in an instant. (Hey, if COVID-19 didn't convince you of this, nothing else will!) You can set your plans in motion, but something crazy can happen to change everything. Graduations get postponed. Schools shut down. Friends can't see each other. . .

Life is unpredictable, for sure. But did you know that those seasons can show who you really are? The way you react to life's chaos reveals a lot—about your character, your faith, or your lack of faith.

God wants you to remain strong, even in the crazy seasons. Keep praying. Keep believing. Keep speaking words of faith. Even if this isn't what you signed up for, it can become something beautiful. (God's in the business of turning chaos into beauty, after all.) If you hang in there, people will see your faith and be drawn to the Lord because of it.

*Lord, I'll stay strong, even when life gets flipped upside down.
I won't give in to fear or defeat. I won't let confusion rob
me of my peace. I'll stick with You, Lord! Amen.*

Hold Up, Lord!

*Think over what I say, for the Lord will
give you understanding in everything.*
2 TIMOTHY 2:7 ESV

Do you ever feel like you're in a maze and can't find the way out? There really are seasons like that, when nothing makes sense. You try and try, but just can't figure out what to do.

Even then, when chaos surrounds you, God wants you to pray and trust in Him. Today's scripture promises that God will give you understanding. . . in everything. Read that again. In everything. There's not a problem too big for Him. There's not a mess too messy for Him. There's not a health problem too complicated for Him. Even when life is at its very worst, God is still at His very best.

Instead of throwing your hands up in the air and saying, "Hold up, Lord!" lift those hands to heaven and say, "Okay, Lord. . .I give up. I can't fix this, but I know You can." Then, do the one thing that will change everything: trust Him. It won't be easy, but if you do, you might just be surprised at how well He handles that crazy situation.

*Lord, I'll place my trust in You. Thank You for giving
me understanding, even in the crazy seasons. Amen.*

It's Too Hard. I Just Can't.

Be happy in your hope. Do not give up when trouble comes.
Do not let anything stop you from praying.
ROMANS 12:12 NLV

"Nope. Not gonna do it. Not today, maybe not ever."

Have you ever spoken those words? There are days when you just can't. Or at least you *feel* like you can't. Here's the funny thing about feelings though . . .they are often deceptive. If you only do what you feel like you can do, then you won't do much.

Today, change your "I can't" to "I can. . .with His help." Say those words and really mean them in your heart of hearts. He can. No matter how big the problem. No matter how deep the valley. No matter how complicated the mess. He can. . .and He will, if you don't stop believing.

Keep your hope alive. Don't give up on the "I can't" days. As today's verse says, "Do not let anything stop you from praying." (Hey, that's what the enemy of your soul wants most of all, to disconnect you from God. Don't let him!)

Lord, I'll stay connected. I'll keep believing. I'll be happy
in my hope, and I won't give up, no matter what! Amen.

My Friend Is Hurting. . .a Lot

Those who are right with the Lord cry, and He hears them.
And He takes them from all their troubles.
PSALM 34:17 NLV

It's breaking your heart to watch. Your friend is going through a crisis, and you can't help her. The situation is out of your control. It's out of hers too. She's heartbroken and completely overwhelmed, and you don't know how to fix this for her.

God placed you in this friend's life for a specific reason. He wants you to stand in the gap for her—to pray about her situation, her heart, and her emotions. Pray for her strength, her hope, her joy. Then let her know that you are going to be there for her, no matter how things turn out.

She's going to need you, that's for sure. So keep yourself strong. Be ready to listen when she needs to talk. And always speak words of hope over her situation so she doesn't give up. (This is only possible if you're actually filled with hope yourself.)

Most of all, trust God with your friend. Believe it or not, He loves her even more than you do.

Lord, I've been so worried about my friend. I'm trusting You to get
her through this. Show me what I can do to help, I pray. Amen.

Life Isn't Fair!

I called to the Lord in my trouble. I cried to God for help. He heard my voice from His holy house. My cry for help came into His ears.
PSALM 18:6 NLV

"That's not fair!" How many times would you guess the average human uses those words in the span of a lifetime? It starts when we're toddlers, and our sibling gets something we think we deserve. Then it escalates as we get older and we don't get our way. It moves into adulthood as life causes upsets and complications that interfere with our plans. Any time we don't get what we want (or think we deserve), we cry out, "Hey, that's not fair!"

The thing is, no one ever said life was going to be fair. If it were, then why did Jesus—who lived a sinless life—have to go to the cross and die for us sinners?

No, it's not fair. But one thing you can be sure of—God is there in the unfair moments. You can cry out to Him and He will hear and respond out of His great love for you. You might not always get the answers you're seeking—He's not a genie in a bottle, after all—but He will usually surprise you with something even better.

Lord, I'm ready to give up my "It's not fair" speech. I'm counting on You to give me Your very best, whatever that looks like. Amen.

Sometimes I Get Mad!

If you are angry, do not let it become sin.
Get over your anger before the day is finished.
EPHESIANS 4:26 NLV

Aargh! Sometimes your anger reaches the boiling point! You want to punch something. Or yell at someone. Or stomp your foot. Anything to get the feelings out.

Did you know that anger isn't a sin? (Hey, even Jesus got angry!) No, it's what you *do* with that anger that matters to God. When you get mad, it's important to cool down before it begins to affect your actions. Don't let it become sin.

This is where a lot of girls go wrong. They get angry. They react. Things escalate. God's heart is broken and the situation gets worse instead of better. Get over your anger before the day is done. (Hint: don't go to bed angry.) Let the bomb in your heart diffuse so that it doesn't explode and accidentally hurt everyone who happens to be nearby.

Lord, I'll admit. . .sometimes I let my anger boil over. I act on it and I always regret it. Things get worse, not better. Today I'll count to ten. I'll diffuse the bomb. I won't let it go off. But I'll need Your help with this, for sure! Amen.

Date:

DEAR GOD, ...
....
....
....

I'm thankful for. . . ..
....
....
....
....
....
....
....

My worries. . . ..
....
....
....
....
....

People I am praying for. . . ..
....
....
....
....
....

Here's what's going on in my life. . .

MY NEEDS. . .

Other stuff I need to share
with You, God. . .

AMEN.
Thank You, Father,
for hearing my prayers.

WEEK 11

I Blew It, Lord!

"Watch and pray so that you will not be tempted. Man's spirit is willing, but the body does not have the power to do it."
MATTHEW 26:41 NLV

Have you ever tried to print something only to discover the printer was running out of ink? You can still sort of see the text on the page, but you have to squint to make it out.

Sometimes our prayer life can get like that. Our spiritual ink cartridge runs dry. We still go through the motions, but we're not as tuned in to God as we used to be. Maybe we wonder if He can read what we're putting on the page at all or if He even cares. And because we give up on Him, we start slipping up. We blow it—in our relationships, our work ethic, even our prayer time.

God has supernatural 20/20 vision. He sees the hidden places in your heart and He knows when you're struggling. Don't ever be afraid to go to Him when your well has run dry. He promises to fill you up and to make your picture bright again. And by the way. . .He can still read the text on the pages of your heart and knows when you're blowing it anyway!

Lord, my well runs dry sometimes. Today I need You to fill me up. Make the pages of my heart fully readable, I pray. Amen.

I Blew It with My Parents

Children, obey your parents in the Lord, for this is right. "Honor your
father and mother" (this is the first commandment with a promise),
"that it may go well with you and that you may live long in the land."
Fathers, do not provoke your children to anger, but bring them
up in the discipline and instruction of the Lord.
EPHESIANS 6:1–4 ESV

You didn't mean for it to happen, but it did. You blew up at your parents. You said things you now regret. You could tell from the shocked look on your mom's face that some of your words stung. They hurt her heart. And you have mixed feelings about that because you meant for them to. Only now you feel bad. You wish you could take it all back. Can you still make things right?

It's never too late to make things right, whether you've hurt your parents, a good friend, or a sibling. The desire to want to fix things is where it starts. But next you have to act on that desire. There are twelve words that can fix any relationship: *I am sorry. I was wrong. Please forgive me. I love you.* Those words will truly fix any broken situation.

Lord, give me courage to face my parents and
make apologies for what I've done. Amen.

I Blew It with My Friend

Know this, my beloved brothers: let every person
be quick to hear, slow to speak, slow to anger.
JAMES 1:19 ESV

You're feeling pretty down in the dumps about what you said to your friend. You didn't mean to hurt him. . .but you did. Several days have passed, and he's still not responding to your texts or taking your calls. And that time you passed him in the hall at school, he turned his head and looked the other way.

If only you could go back, have a re-do on the conversation. The mean words just slipped out. In fact, you thought they were funny. He didn't laugh, though. And he's still not laughing.

In situations like this, there's only one way to fix the problem. You have to be 100 percent on board with a genuine apology and a commitment not to do it again. Then if the wall between you is too big, you take a step back and allow God to work on your friend's heart while you continue to pray that the situation will turn around.

These things usually work themselves out with time. Do the right thing. Be patient. Pray. Trust God.

Lord, I'm asking You to fix this broken relationship. Please! Amen.

I Blew It with My Schoolwork

The lazy man does not plow before winter.
So he begs during gathering time and has nothing.
PROVERBS 20:4 NLV

You didn't mean to push the assignment off to the very last minute. Your intentions were good. But your follow-through? Not so much. Now it's the night before you have to turn in the project and you're not even close. There's no one but yourself to blame, so there's no way you can point fingers. Now what? How do you get through this?

First, deep breath. Don't spend a lot of time wishing things were different or wallowing in regret. Ask for God's forgiveness and then His patience and help. Do the best you can, and then turn in the project, regardless of what it looks like. This might be one of those tough life lessons you're always hearing about. It will teach you how to handle the situation better next time.

You *will* do better next time, as long as you stay aware and on top of things. Don't beat yourself up. Just keep going.

Lord, I'm sorry I didn't follow through the way I should have!
Please forgive me, and shower me with grace and courage
so I can get as much done as I can. I need You! Amen.

I Blew It with My Attitude

"Do not let us be tempted, but keep us from sin."
MATTHEW 6:13 NLV

Oh boy. That attitude, girl! You sure know how to use it, don't you? You can sling it around like mud, hitting its intended target. The problem is, you show it off in front of others and (just keeping it real) it doesn't look pretty on you. In fact, it shows off the ugliness inside your heart.

You want to change that attitude? Start by acknowledging it, then truly repenting for it. After that, submit to the Lord and ask Him to change you from the inside out. Once that is done—once your heart is fully His—then that attitude won't come flying out next time. No, next time you'll be more patient, loving, and gracious. You'll also be quicker to do what's being asked of you.

Attitude check! Don't let life's temptations cause you to sin.

Lord, I'll admit it. . .I've got a lousy attitude sometimes.
My parents aren't the only ones who see it. I've been showing
it off all over town. But no more! Today I give my heart
(and my attitudes) fully to You. Change me, I pray. Amen.

Am I Destined to Mess Up Everything?

When he falls, he will not be thrown down,
because the Lord holds his hand.
PSALM 37:24 NLV

You feel like such a loser sometimes, don't you? It's like everything you touch ends up messed up or broken. Truthfully, you almost reach the giving-up point sometimes. Why bother trying when everything turns out to be such a mess?

Girl, you need a change of thinking! Those "just give it up" thoughts don't come from God. He wants you to keep trying, no matter how many mess-ups or slipups you go through. And He's certainly not beating you up for your mistakes.

Today's verse makes it plain: when you fall, you won't be abandoned by God. He's not looking at you and saying, "Good grief, this one's such a mess!" Instead, He reaches down, grabs your hand, and says, "Get up, girl. We've got work to do. The next time, things will go better."

Things *will* get better, you know. They really will. So don't give up. Plenty of glorious adventures lie ahead.

Lord, I won't give up. Thank You for holding
my hand and lifting me up when I fall. Amen.

Date:

DEAR GOD, ...

I'm thankful for. . . ..

My worries. . . ..

People I am praying for. . . ..

Here's what's going on in my life. . .

MY NEEDS. . .

Other stuff I need to share with You, God. . .

AMEN.
Thank You, Father, for hearing my prayers.

WEEK 12
Fix It, Lord!

He heals the brokenhearted and binds up their wounds.
PSALM 147:3 ESV

How good are you at fixing things? Some girls just have a knack for mechanical stuff. A broken bike. A busted laptop. A leaky faucet. No problem! And when it comes to the big things—broken relationships, broken hearts, broken spirits. . .they just seem to know how to put them back together again. You wonder how they got such amazing skills and wish you had a few of those yourself.

Here's the really cool thing about hanging out with God: He's the best fix-it person available. There's nothing broken that He cannot repair. There's nothing too far gone. Absolutely nothing is impossible with Him.

Are you struggling with a broken relationship? No problem. He can fix it. Broken spirit? He can fix that too. Are you struggling with a class at school? He can take care of that one as well. There's literally nothing you can name that He cannot fix. So instead of giving up, spend some time today saying these four words: "Please fix it, Lord!"

Lord, that's all I can think to say today as I stare at the mess around me: "Please fix it, Lord!" Amen.

Fix the Deepest Parts of Me

*The sacrifices of God are a broken spirit; a broken
and contrite heart, O God, you will not despise.*

PSALM 51:17 ESV

You're broken, way down deep. The cracks are so tiny, so well hidden, that no one even knows they're there. You plaster a smile on your face and pretend everything's okay, but it's really not. Inside, your heart is breaking. And you wonder how long you can go on faking it.

God sees those microscopic breaks in your heart, girl. He wants you to bring them to the surface so He can fully heal them. It starts with opening up and confessing your pain. Take it to God. He's big enough to handle it. He'll take those tiny cracks and seal them back up again, making them stronger than ever.

Think of how a scar heals. The skin grows up around the cut and makes the area tougher to penetrate next time. That's how it is with your broken heart. God will toughen it up so you're not so easily broken next time around. But it all starts with giving it to Him, so He can do the work to make things better now.

*Lord, I come to You today with my (very) broken heart.
Fix the broken places, I pray. Amen.*

Fix These Icky Feelings

Keep your heart with all vigilance,
for from it flow the springs of life.
PROVERBS 4:23 ESV

You can't really put your finger on it, but you're having an "off" day. Nothing feels right. There's a nagging feeling in your heart, one you can't shake. It's bothered you all day. Maybe it's that broken friendship still troubling you. Or maybe it's the medical test your mom is going through. Could be that big test you bombed in science. There's a lot going on.

It's not always easy to pinpoint those weird, troubling feelings, but here's a fact: God is the Keeper of your heart. He wants it to remain strong, even on the "off" days. That doesn't mean He wants you to fake it; just that He wants you to give it to Him.

Keep that heart safe, girl. Don't get overwhelmed with bad feelings. Shake them off as quickly as you can so that you don't get bogged down. There are too many great things going on out there to spend too much time fretting over icky feelings.

Lord, take this heart today, I pray. Fix these troubling
feelings. I trust You, the Keeper of my heart. Amen.

Fix These Awkward Relationships

*With all humility and gentleness, with patience,
bearing with one another in love, eager to
maintain the unity of the Spirit in the bond of peace.*
Ephesians 4:2–3 esv

Some of your relationships are just. . .awkward. You know the ones. Whenever you're around that particular person, you just tense up. You're not yourself. You try too hard. . .or you don't try at all. You wish things were easier, but this one seems destined to remain awkward forever.

Some friendships really are tense like that, but most get better with time if they're meant to be. (And let's face it, not every friendship is going to be long-term. Sometimes it's better to back away from the fire before you get burned.)

Still, God is the fixer of relationships. He can make those awkward feelings go away if you pray about them. He can show you how to be the best possible friend without losing pieces of yourself along the way. (There's nothing worse than sacrificing who you really are just to make someone like you, after all!)

*Lord, I've got this one friend. You know the one.
Things with her are just. . .weird. Fix it, please? Amen.*

Fix the Unfair Stuff!

*I cried to Him with my mouth and
praised Him with my tongue.*
PSALM 66:17 NLV

It's not fair! You've been asked to do something that isn't yours to do. And you're mad about it. Who wouldn't be? Still, you have no choice, so you follow through. . .but with an angry heart. You didn't make this mess. Why do you have to be the one to clean it up?

Life will give you plenty of opportunities to get upset about having to do other people's work. And you're right. . .it's not fair. But the truth is, if you don't do it, the job probably won't get done. Maybe you've been asked to perform this task because you've proven in the past that you're a girl who follows through. Because you've proven you're responsible, your mom—or your boss—now calls on you to pick up the slack from someone else's mistake.

It isn't fair. But if you keep going, if you do the task that's been set in front of you, God can use it to promote you and to shine a light on your good attitude. (Hey, maybe you'll even get a promotion at work if you keep this up!)

*Lord, these unfair moments seem to happen a lot.
Work on my heart so I'm not resentful, I pray. Amen.*

Fix This Broken World

Therefore God has highly exalted him and bestowed on him the name that is above every name, so that at the name of Jesus every knee should bow, in heaven and on earth and under the earth, and every tongue confess that Jesus Christ is Lord, to the glory of God the Father.

PHILIPPIANS 2:9–11 ESV

Wars. Rumors of wars. Persecution of Christians around the globe. Sex trafficking. Slavery. Abuse. Across this great planet, troubles abound. You could point to any country on the map and news stories of the tragedies in that place would greet you.

So what's a girl to do? It's hard not to get depressed about all the sadness (and badness) going on in the world today.

During those moments when it starts to feel overwhelming, remember today's scripture. One day every knee on the planet will bow. Every single person (male, female, all ethnicities) will proclaim that Jesus is Lord. Until then, your job is to pray. Never stop praying, in fact. This world desperately needs your intercession.

Lord, I pray for the broken people, broken governments, and broken homes across the globe. Fix this broken world, I pray. Amen.

Date

DEAR GOD, ...
....
....
....

I'm thankful for. . . ..
....
....
....
....
....
....
....

My worries. . . ..
....
....
....
....
....

People I am praying for. . ...
....
....
....
....

Here's what's going on in my life. . .

MY NEEDS. . .

Other stuff I need to share with You, God. . .

AMEN.
Thank You, Father,
for hearing my prayers.

WEEK 13
The World's Gone Crazy!

If we say we have no sin, we deceive ourselves, and the truth is not in us. If we confess our sins, he is faithful and just to forgive us our sins and to cleanse us from all unrighteousness. If we say we have not sinned, we make him a liar, and his word is not in us.

1 JOHN 1:8–10 ESV

They've gone crazy out there, haven't they? It seems people are always bickering or fighting about something. Politics. Religion. Race. You name it, they're fighting over it. And you're stuck in the middle. You want to shout, "Hey, could you stop arguing long enough to have a normal conversation?" But they don't seem to want to talk sensibly. It's more exciting for them to have a shouting match.

But you're done with the arguments. You don't want to do it the world's way anymore. You're ready to do it God's way. So you settle down your heart. You give your emotions a rest. And you run to Jesus with the words, "Lord, help me remain pure in this crazy world!" on your lips.

He will, you know. The rest of the world might be doing it their own way, but when you submit to the authority of Christ in your life, He cleanses you and places you on the right path. So run to Him today. He's got a better way for you.

Lord, I don't want to do it the world's way. I've tried that, and it didn't work. Today I'm coming to You for answers. . .no one else. Amen.

Upside-Down Messages

He wants all people to be saved from the punishment of sin.
He wants them to come to know the truth.
1 TIMOTHY 2:4 NLV

Remember when right was right and wrong was wrong? You could clearly see with your own eyes when something was "off" and say, "Um, no. . .that's just wrong." But these days it's getting harder and harder to speak truth. People claim there are no absolutes—and what used to be wrong is now right, and what used to be right is now wrong. . .and you feel dazed and confused.

Your friends are joining in the fun in this upside-down world, calling sin okay. You don't want to be a joiner, but they're making it hard. They're calling you names and implying that if you don't join them in their beliefs that means you don't love people as much as they do.

Only, you *do* love people as much as they do, and perhaps more. Because you're concerned about their souls, not just their actions. So you do the one thing that makes the most sense. . .you pray. You give it all to Jesus, the only One big enough to handle it all.

I want to do things Your way, Lord—the right-side-up way! Amen.

Politics. . .Ugh!

Pray for kings and all others who are in power over us so we might live quiet God-like lives in peace. It is good when you pray like this. It pleases God Who is the One Who saves.

1 TIMOTHY 2:2–3 NLV

Whole families are split apart over politics these days. Which candidate to vote for. Whether to be conservative or liberal. Whether to tear down statues or leave them up. Whether to change the country's belief system or keep it the same.

Everywhere you look, people are walking away from their friends and loved ones over politics. But does this make God's heart happy? Is He pleased when people put their political beliefs over relationships?

This is a tricky subject, isn't it? God wants you to stick to your convictions, but He's also keen on living together in harmony with others. So before you walk away from any relationships, pray about it. Ask God to show you His way through this crazy, topsy-turvy political season we're living in.

Lord, I don't want to see people separated over politics. Can you mend relationships and show us the way forward? Please?

My Friends Are Headed the Wrong Way

*Do not let anyone fool you. Bad people can make
those who want to live good become bad.*

1 Corinthians 15:33 nlv

Your heart is broken over some of your friends. The decisions they've made have been bad ones. You tried to warn them, but they wouldn't listen. Now they're in a mess. . .but don't seem to realize it. They don't even notice how lost they are.

How do you handle tough situations like that? When people deny that their bad actions are bad. . .then what? Do you close your eyes to it? Pretend they're telling the truth? Ignore their behaviors? Do you rat them out to the teacher or their parents? What's the right answer?

The best thing you can do for your friend is to back away from the situation and pray. Commit yourself to pray diligently for him. Ask God to reveal truth. And if the opportunity presents itself, you speak truthfully—whether it's directly to him or to an adult who's asking questions about his behavior. Better to tell the truth in love than to join in the lie. Lies only lead to death, after all.

*Lord, this is tricky. I hate to see my friends fall so far
away from You. Show me what to do, please. Amen.*

A Jumbled Mess

*God knows the hearts of men. He knows what the
Holy Spirit is thinking. The Holy Spirit prays for those
who belong to Christ the way God wants Him to pray.*
ROMANS 8:27 NLV

Do you get confused when you hear the mixed messages the world puts out through movies, books, and TV shows? They want to change your thinking about so many things and expect you to switch over to their way of believing. It's easy to get confused. And it doesn't help when your friends cave and start believing the world's way.

God knows the confusion going on inside your heart. He sees the wrestling match. And He's showing you, even now, how to focus and stay true to Him. The Holy Spirit is hard at work inside of you, praying when you don't know how to pray. Guiding you when you don't know the right way to go. Leading you in the direction that will please God's heart and lead to a healthy outcome.

Trust the work going on inside of you, even when everything around you is a jumbled mess. God is bigger!

*Lord, I trust You to keep working things out,
even when I'm very (very!) confused. Amen.*

Do They See You in Me?

*"When you pray, do not be as those who pretend to be someone
they are not. They love to stand and pray in the places of
worship or in the streets so people can see them. For sure,
I tell you, they have all the reward they are going to get."*

MATTHEW 6:5 NLV

God has called you to be a light-bearer. You are to be a city on a hill, a shining reflection of Him.

That's easier said than done, isn't it? These days, it's tempting to go along with the crowd. They all believe certain things that don't line up with the Bible, and you're tempted to join in because of peer pressure.

But you don't. You keep standing strong. You still treat them in a loving way, the way Jesus has taught you to. But you wonder. . .do they see Jesus in you or do they just see you as different? Weird?

Hang in there, girl. Don't give up. There's a reward for those who stand strong. Don't cave to those who would try to change you. And don't be a hypocrite—one way with your friends and another way at home and church. You just be a shining reflection of Him, no matter who you're with.

I'm trying, Lord! I want to shine for You. Amen.

Date:

DEAR GOD, ...
....
....
....

I'm thankful for. . . ..
....
....
....
....
....
....
....

My worries. . . ..
....
....
....
....
....

People I am praying for. . . ..
....
....
....
....

Here's what's going on in my life. . .

MY NEEDS. . .

Other stuff I need to share with You, God. . .

AMEN.
Thank You, Father,
for hearing my prayers.

WEEK 14

Education Matters

The fear of the LORD is the beginning of knowledge;
fools despise wisdom and instruction.
PROVERBS 1:7 ESV

There's a difference between head knowledge and heart knowledge. There's also a difference between knowledge (the world's version) and wisdom (God-knowledge). But here's the truth: you need all of it. You need the kind of knowledge you can get in school—all those subjects in all those classes. And you need the wisdom of God to go along with it.

You will be on a learning curve your whole life, girl. But that's kind of the point. God is shaping and molding you, so He wants you to be pliable in His hands. Maybe that's why today's verse says that fools despise wisdom and instruction. Because they're not usable to God when they refuse to learn the lessons He's teaching them.

You, though? You're an A+ student when it comes to learning the kinds of lessons He is teaching you. So hang in there. You'll be at the top of your class before long, if you don't give up.

Lord, I commit to being a faithful student
all the days of my life. Amen.

Educating My Spirit

How much better to get wisdom than gold! To get understanding is to be chosen rather than silver.
PROVERBS 16:16 ESV

Have you ever known someone who was book smart but didn't seem to know anything about the Lord. . .at all? Crazy, isn't it? Some people can have all the knowledge in the world, but they still seem closed off to the Gospel message.

Maybe this is why God is so keen on educating the spirit, not just the mind. Today's verse says it's better to get wisdom than gold. (I know, I know! You want both!) But when you get understanding (heavenly wisdom) you really have everything you need for a productive life. So choose that above all else.

And while you're at it, pray for those friends who are head-smart but not God-smart. Pray that the eyes of their understanding will be opened to the truth. Once they open themselves up to that, anything can (and will!) happen.

Lord, I trust You with my book-smart friends. I want them to have a relationship with You, so I'll keep praying for them until true wisdom penetrates their hearts. Amen.

Educating My Heart

As in water face reflects face,
so the heart of man reflects the man.
PROVERBS 27:19 ESV

Isn't today's verse an amazing one? You look into the water and see the reflection of your face (though perhaps a little blurry). In the same way, your heart is a real reflection of the true you.

That sounds good until someone gets you worked up. You come out swinging, saying some ugly things. Ugh. "Out of the abundance of the heart the mouth speaks" (Matthew 12:34 ESV). There's no denying that reflection, is there?

It's time to educate your heart. And there's really only one way to do that. Get in the Word. Stay in the Word. Memorize the Word. Make the Bible a priority. Keep it close by. Come up with a plan to commit verses to memory so that the only thing flying out of your heart during rough seasons is the Word of God.

You can also educate your heart by keeping it open to the Holy Spirit. He's moving in and through you, even now. Allow yourself to be used by Him to reach others and that heart will stay nice and soft.

Lord, I commit myself to Your heart-education system! Amen.

Educating My Mind

Do not be conformed to this world, but be transformed by the renewal of your mind, that by testing you may discern what is the will of God, what is good and acceptable and perfect.
ROMANS 12:2 ESV

The Bible tells us not to be conformed to this world. Think about it. You pour water into a glass and it takes the shape of the glass you pour it into. If we're not careful, the same thing can happen to us. We become like everyone—and everything—around us. We take on their shape.

But God wants you to train your mind so that you can keep your God-shape 24/7, 365 days a year. It's not always easy, but it is possible.

Don't conform. Instead, be transformed. That means you somehow rise above it all. You ask God to take charge of your thoughts, to give you His thoughts, not your own. You ask for His will to be done, not yours. And you ask questions like, "Lord, what do You think about this situation? Are my actions pleasing to You?"

When you live like that, transformed thinking is truly possible. Imagine how the world could change if all of us would allow God to transform our minds!

I'm ready, Lord! Transform my thinking! Amen.

Educating My Body

*For while bodily training is of some value, godliness
is of value in every way, as it holds promise for
the present life and also for the life to come.*
1 TIMOTHY 4:8 ESV

Did you know that your body has to be trained? It's true! Think about a gymnast, trying to prepare her body for that next new move. She's got to s-t-r-e-t-c-h those muscles and tendons to prepare them for that eventual split. She can't just jump right into it or she might do some serious damage!

It's the same with you. In the same way you train your mind, you can train your body—to run farther, exercise longer, eat better, even to be more active when you don't feel like it.

You might wonder what this has to do with prayer. Everything! God wants you to be committed to Him—body, soul, and spirit. This means He wants you to bring your body into submission. No sloppy ways for you, girl! Be the best version of you that you can be! It will honor Him when you offer every part of you.

*Lord, there are things in my body that I can change, but I'll need
Your help. I want to be the best version of me I can be. Amen.*

The Learning Goes On. . .Forever!

What you have learned and received and heard and seen in me—practice
these things, and the God of peace will be with you.
PHILIPPIANS 4:9 ESV

As you know, you'll be learning every day of your life for the rest of your life. But here's a cool bit of information you might not have considered: It's not enough just to learn something. You have to apply it to your life and live it out.

Let's say you learned that taking vitamin C could keep you from getting sick. Would it do you any good if you acquired the knowledge but never actually took the vitamin C? Could just knowing keep you healthy? No! You would need to follow through.

The same is true in every area. Follow-through is critical. . .to change your attitude, your actions, and your long-term behaviors. God is looking for the follow-through, not just the knowledge.

Today, take inventory. What areas do you need to pray about? Where have you acquired the knowledge but not carried through? Ask God to reveal a plan of action so you can move forward from here.

I want to practice what I've learned, Lord.
Show me how, I pray. Amen.

Date:

DEAR GOD, ...
....
....
....

I'm thankful for. . . ..
....
....
....
....
....
....
....

My worries. . . ..
....
....
....
....
....
....

People I am praying for. . . ..
....
....
....
....
....

Here's what's going on in my life. . . ..
....
....
....
....

MY NEEDS. . .

....
....
....
....
....
....
....
....
....
....
....
....

Other stuff I need to share
with You, God. . .

....
....
....
....
....
....
....
....

AMEN.
Thank You, Father,
for hearing my prayers.

WEEK 15

Beauty and the Beast

*But the LORD said to Samuel, "Do not look on his appearance
or on the height of his stature, because I have rejected him.
For the LORD sees not as man sees: man looks on the outward
appearance, but the LORD looks on the heart."*

1 SAMUEL 16:7 ESV

. . . .

You've met her—that girl who's beautiful on the outside but a beast on the inside. She wins people over with that gorgeous hair and smile, then shreds them behind their backs. Her heart is exposed over and over again, but people don't seem to notice or care because she's so pretty.

God cares, though. It's one thing to be beautiful on the outside but another to be beautiful on the inside. (In an ideal world, we'd get to be both, right?)

Don't be swayed by that good-looking guy if he's a jerk. Don't be bowled over by that gorgeous friend who's always putting you down. Instead, look for the ones who keep their lives in balance—paying as much attention to the internal as the external. It's a balancing act, for sure, but true beauty always shines through.

. . . .

*Lord, I want to avoid the beasts if I can! And while
I'm at it, I want to avoid becoming one too! Amen.*

Inside Beauty

Don't be concerned about the outward beauty of fancy hairstyles, expensive jewelry, or beautiful clothes. You should clothe yourselves instead with the beauty that comes from within, the unfading beauty of a gentle and quiet spirit, which is so precious to God.

1 PETER 3:3–4 NLT

What comes to your mind when you read the words, "Don't be concerned about the outward beauty of fancy hairstyles, expensive jewelry, or beautiful clothes"? That's a tough one, right? Most girls love that stuff—dressing up, wearing makeup, fixing their hair. In fact, some girls spend hours on their outward appearance.

There's nothing wrong with being lovely, but the point of this verse is to have God's version of beauty that comes from deep within. When you have that kind of beauty, it never fades. The external kind? It's not forever. That firm skin will one day be saggy and wrinkled. That flawless face will one day have age spots. But internal beauty? It's going to last forever. An eternity, in fact!

Lord, I don't want to get so wrapped up in hair, makeup, and clothes that I forget what's really important. Give me ageless internal beauty, I pray! Amen.

A Beautiful Spirit

She opens her mouth with wisdom,
and the teaching of kindness is on her tongue.
PROVERBS 31:26 ESV

Maybe you've heard the expression, "She's got a beautiful spirit!" Usually what people mean when they say something like this is, "She's a really great person—loving and giving." But isn't it interesting that they don't mention how she actually looks (physically). They don't say, "That short girl with the brown hair has a beautiful spirit!" No, when you've got a beautiful spirit, that's pretty much all people notice about you.

So how do you develop a beautiful spirit? By focusing on others, not yourself. By lifting them up in prayer and going out of your way to honor them and treat them well. Having a beautiful spirit also means you treat all people with respect, the way you would want to be treated.

Who knew it was so easy to be beautiful? Just do things God's way, and before long you'll be a true beauty queen.

Lord, I want to have a beautiful spirit.
Help me to be others-focused, I pray. Amen.

Seeing the Beauty in Others

Love is patient and kind; love does not envy or boast; it is not arrogant.

1 CORINTHIANS 13:4 ESV

Have you ever had a friend who was so loving, so kind, that you couldn't help but love her back? Maybe she wasn't like the other girls you hung out with, but her kindness made her irresistible.

God wants the world to be filled with irresistibly beautiful people like that—the kind that win over others to their heart. You can be that kind of girl too. It will require something big of you though—noticing others. *Really* noticing them. Notice what they're going through. Notice when they do something right. Notice when they're hurting.

And pray for those girls you're noticing. You don't have to make a big deal out of it, but simply say, "Hey, I've been praying for you." Those words will make you irresistible to her. She'll be astounded that you took the time to lift her up in prayer.

Seeing the beauty in others is easy when the beauty of the Lord resides in your heart. So pour it out, girl!

Lord, I want to be the kind of girl who truly notices others. Help me with that, I pray. Amen.

Discovering the Beauty of You

I praise you, for I am fearfully and wonderfully made.
Wonderful are your works; my soul knows it very well.
PSALM 139:14 ESV

If someone asked, "What do you see in yourself that's beautiful?" how would you respond? Maybe you would say, "Well, my ears are cute." Or, "I think I've got a fine nose." No doubt, you would come back with something about your physical appearance. You were created in the image of God, so it's nice to notice the things you like about your physique.

Beyond all of that though. . .what is lovely about you? Your attitude? Your heart toward those who are struggling? Your passion for missions? Your kindness to the girls others overlook?

There are so many ways to be beautiful. Today, take inventory. Find your weaknesses and strengths. Then pray and ask God to show you how you can further develop that beauty for all to see.

You've created me to be beautiful, Lord. Show me how I can
fully develop that beauty to reach this world for You. Amen.

Beautiful in His Time

He has made everything beautiful in its time. Also, he has put eternity into man's heart, yet so that he cannot find out what God has done from the beginning to the end.
ECCLESIASTES 3:11 ESV

It might not seem beautiful now. . .that situation you're dealing with. But don't you love the promise that God will make all things beautiful in His time? So if a situation isn't lovely yet. . .just wait. It will be. If a relationship isn't coming together as you'd hoped, hang in there. He can still make something gorgeous out of it.

The problem with human beings is we want everything perfect right away. But some things just take time. Think about a wedding cake. It's not very pretty when it's just eggs and sugar and flour in a bowl. The individual layers of cake aren't even very tempting. But when the baker starts to assemble those layers and then adds the icing and décor. . .wow! It all comes together.

Think of your life like that cake. Things are still coming together. God hasn't added the icing yet. But just wait. . .it's coming!

Lord, I can't wait to see how things turn out! Thanks for making everything beautiful in Your time. Amen.

Date:

DEAR GOD, _____
_____
_____
_____

I'm thankful for. . . _____
_____
_____
_____
_____
_____
_____
_____

My worries. . . _____
_____
_____
_____
_____
_____

People I am praying for. . . _____
_____
_____
_____
_____

Here's what's going on in my life. . .

MY NEEDS. . .

Other stuff I need to share with You, God. . .

AMEN.
Thank You, Father,
for hearing my prayers.

WEEK 16

Believing for the Big Stuff

Jesus said to them, "For sure, I tell you this: If you have faith and do not doubt, you will not only be able to do what was done to the fig tree. You will also be able to say to this mountain, 'Move from here and be thrown into the sea,' and it will be done. All things you ask for in prayer, you will receive if you have faith."

MATTHEW 21:21–22 NLV

How long does it take you to do a project for school? Days, right? Or depending on how complicated the project is, maybe even weeks. Does it boggle your mind to realize that God made the entire universe and everything in it in one week's time? He can do in one second what it would take us months or even years to do. (Not that any of us could actually create the universe, but you get the idea.)

He's magnificent, awe-inspiring, and capable of ten-million-times more than we could ever dream. So why do we ever doubt him? If He did all of that—flung the stars into the night sky, caused the rivers to rush downstream, placed all the planets together just so—think of what He can do for you! Don't be afraid to ask the Creator of everything for His help in your life.

You've done it all, Lord! How could I help but trust You?

Unanswered Prayers

And this is the confidence that we have toward him,
that if we ask anything according to his will he hears us.
1 JOHN 5:14 ESV

A banana is a wonderful piece of fruit. . .until it isn't. It doesn't take very long for a banana to get speckled on the outside and mushy on the inside. You have to eat one when it's just right.

In some ways, life is like a banana. You go through seasons where you feel like you're ready but you're not quite ripe yet. Then you go through other seasons where you know you're ready for a big task but no one will give you an opportunity. If you sit on the shelf long enough, you'll get speckled and spoiled! Don't they see that?

Here's the really cool news about God: He knows the best timing for absolutely everything going on in your life. He knows when to give you an opportunity and when to hold back. You can trust God with the timing of everything. So don't give up when those prayers aren't answered in a hurry. The answer is on the way. . .in His time.

Lord, I will trust You with the timing. Amen.

Hey, God. . .Did You Forget Me?

Because he has loved Me, I will bring him out of trouble. I will set him in a safe place on high, because he has known My name. He will call upon Me, and I will answer him. I will be with him in trouble. I will take him out of trouble and honor him. I will please him with a long life. And I will show him My saving power.

PSALM 91:14–16 NLV

You pray. . .and pray. And then you pray some more. You don't give up. But it doesn't seem like God's doing much about your situation.

Then you read a verse like this. It's a promise that God will bring you out of trouble and set you in a safe, high place, far above the madness. And you wonder, "When, Lord? When will You do that?"

In His perfect timing. That's when. And believe it or not, God is never late. Oh, it might seem like He is, but He's working all things together in His perfect timing. If only you could see what's going on behind the scenes right now. You'd really be wowed!

Lord, I'll trust that You're working behind the scenes. Thank You for lifting me from my troubles, no matter the timing. Amen.

I Keep Asking. I Keep Knocking.

*"I say to you, ask, and what you ask for will be given to you.
Look, and what you are looking for you will find. Knock,
and the door you are knocking on will be opened to you."*

LUKE 11:9 NLV

Have you ever knocked on a friend's door and then waited. . .and waited. . .and waited? Sometimes the people on the other side of the door simply don't hear you. So you end up ringing the bell. Finally! Someone shows up and lets you in.

God isn't like that. You don't have to keep knocking or ringing the bell. Today's verse offers a promise—knock and the door will open up. Ask and He will respond. Seek and you will find.

In other words, God sees, hears, and reacts to His kids. He doesn't turn and walk the other way when He knows you're at the door. He's listening carefully to your prayers and working on your behalf to bring the best possible answers to the problems you're facing.

Keep asking! Keep seeking! Keep knocking! Never give up on God because He's never given up on you.

*I'm here, Lord—asking, seeking, and knocking.
Thanks for being a responsive God. Amen.*

I Won't Give Up

*Jesus told them a picture-story to show that
men should always pray and not give up.*
LUKE 18:1 NLV

Have you ever been in a really hot, humid place that didn't have air-conditioning? It's miserable, isn't it? No one likes to be uncomfortable.

Unfortunately, you're going to go through many experiences in life that are uncomfortable. They might even make you question whether or not God is paying attention to your situation. He is! And He's growing you, even in the struggles.

Whether it's a relational issue, school related, or even something to do with your family, you can trust God. This uncomfortable situation won't last forever. Instead of whining and complaining about it, pray and ask the Lord for His perspective on what's going on. Chances are pretty good He's working on something miraculous behind the scenes, something that will be revealed at a later date.

Never ever give up. It's simply not an option.

*Lord, I feel like giving up sometimes, but I won't. I'll stick
with You and trust that You're up to something good.*

You Will Use It for Good

*"As for you, you meant evil against me, but God meant
it for good, to bring it about that many people
should be kept alive, as they are today."*
GENESIS 50:20 ESV

Some people have bad motives. Oh, they might appear to be good people on the surface. Friendly, even. In fact, some might cozy up to you and pretend to be really good, trustworthy friends. But then you find out they've been terrible friends, even talking behind your back. Ugh! That can hurt, and it can also make you distrust people. You want to walk away from all relationships and say, "People are just no good!" But you don't, because in your heart you know better.

Here's a fun fact: God can take anything, even the ugly things others have done to you, and use them for His glory. He can bring good from it. If He can place a tiny dry seed in the ground and grow it into a gorgeous tree, then imagine what He can do in your heart.

*I'm counting on it, Lord! They've tried to use words
and actions against me, but You're turning it around
even now. I'll trust You with the process! Amen.*

Date:

DEAR GOD, ...
....
....
....

I'm thankful for. . . ..
....
....
....
....
....
....
....

My worries. . . ..
....
....
....
....
....

People I am praying for. . . ..
....
....
....
....
....

Here's what's going on in my life. . .

MY NEEDS. . .

Other stuff I need to share
with You, God. . .

AMEN.
Thank You, Father,
for hearing my prayers.

WEEK 17

You Are Holy

"Pray like this: 'Our Father in heaven, Your name is holy.' "
MATTHEW 6:9 NLV

You never know what you're going to get when you buy a watermelon, do you? Sometimes you cut into it and it looks perfect on the inside but tastes nasty! Other times it looks perfect on the outside, then you cut into it and it's not even red inside. In other words, looks can be deceiving.

That's one cool thing about God: what you see is what you get. He's exactly the same yesterday, today, and forever. Perfect on the outside, perfect on the inside, He will never let you down. You can trust Him with your problems, your worries, your relationships, even all that personal stuff you don't like to talk about.

God is holy. He's perfect. And He's completely and totally trustworthy. (Aren't you glad?)

Lord, I trust You, my holy, perfect Father!
You never change. I can always count on You. Amen.

Born to Worship

*"God is spirit, and those who worship
him must worship in spirit and truth."*
JOHN 4:24 ESV

Did you realize that you were created by God to worship Him? It's true! The Bible says that God is spirit and we must all worship him in spirit and truth. But what does that mean exactly? How do you go about worshipping a spirit?

First, acknowledge that He is God and you are not. This might sound silly, but half the time we play the role of God in our own lives—making decisions without consulting Him in prayer or in His Word.

Second, admit that you need a Savior. Give your heart fully to Him. Then remain in a submitted, humble position, always remembering that He created everything. If He created it all, then He must know how it works. He knows the inner workings of your heart and wants the absolute best for you.

Finally, trust Him completely. He's never let you down, and He's not going to start now. Praise Him wholeheartedly, not just for the things He's done but for all He's going to do. God is worthy of your praise and adoration!

*I worship You, Lord—on good days and bad.
You are King of kings and Lord of lords! Amen.*

Holy Moments

May my prayer be like special perfume before You. May the lifting up of my hands be like the evening gift given on the altar in worship.
PSALM 141:2 NLV

You can't stop sniffing the air around you. Someone is wearing perfume or lotion that has a wonderful scent. You want to figure out what it is so that you can buy the same product and use it yourself.

When you're around someone with a yummy aroma, it's a pleasant sensation. But have you ever been around someone who didn't bathe? Or maybe a youngster who's been playing out in the sun? Sometimes that aroma can be pretty bad.

God longs for you to put out a pleasant aroma so that other people will be drawn to you. Oh, not the kind you can buy in a perfume bottle. He's talking about the kind that comes from a deeper place inside your heart. When you are pleasing and loving to others, they will want to be around you. Today, spend time with Jesus and allow Him to soak you in His presence.

I want to be a lovely fragrance to draw others to You, Jesus! Amen.

As You Are Holy. . .

Tell your sins to each other. And pray for each other so you may be healed.
The prayer from the heart of a man right with God has much power.
JAMES 5:16 NLV

When you read the words, "tell your sins to each other," who comes to mind? Who do you envision yourself sharing your sins with? This can be a challenge, finding just the right accountability partner. You want someone who will understand, but not so understanding that they say, "It's okay. No biggie." You want someone tough, but not so tough that they say, "You're a terrible, horrible, no good, very bad person!" You want someone with discernment, who sees things the way God does. And you also want that person to be at least as spiritually mature as you are. (Hey, it would make no sense to take your troubles to an unsaved friend. She would just pat you on the back and say, "Great job!")

Today, ask the Lord to show you who you can trust as a confidant. Then make a pact with your friend that you'll be honest with each other about how you're doing—what areas you're struggling in, and so on. It's always good to have someone else in your corner.

I'm so grateful I don't have to do this alone, Lord! Amen.

Holy Responses to Your Surroundings

On the glorious splendor of your majesty,
and on your wondrous works, I will meditate.
PSALM 145:5 ESV

Sometimes you only talk to God when you're upset about something—like when someone hurts your feelings or when you don't get what you ask for. You forget to go to Him about the things you're okay with.

Like what, you ask? Like sunsets and beaches. Babies with rosy cheeks and puppies that lick your toes. Rivers and mountain peaks, rainy days and fluffy clouds. Friends with bright smiles and family members who adore you. There are so many things you're okay with. And it's a good idea to thank God for those things (especially when you're upset about other things). It's a great reminder that the good outweighs the bad.

It does, you know. But good or bad, you can take it all to Him. He loves hearing from you—whether you're praising Him for the good or wondering about the bad.

Thank You for reminding me that the good outweighs the bad, Lord!

Holy Thoughts

*Christian brothers, keep your minds thinking about whatever
is true, whatever is respected, whatever is right, whatever is pure,
whatever can be loved, and whatever is well thought of. If there is
anything good and worth giving thanks for, think about these things.*
PHILIPPIANS 4:8 NLV

God doesn't just want your actions to be pure; He longs for your thoughts to be pure as well. This can be tough. It's easy to pretend everything's cool on the outside while hiding a dirty heart on the inside. But God sees straight through to that heart, and He's not having any of that. He wants your purity to run from the inside out.

This includes the way you think. His desire is for your thoughts to be pure. This can be particularly tough in your teens when you're hyper-focused on the opposite sex. But even in your quest to find that perfect guy (hint: there's no such thing), you can keep your thoughts pure. And when you do find a guy who's godly and kind, you'll be a good match because he's been keeping his heart and mind pure too.

Think on lovely things. Think on true things. Think on respectable things . . .things that are good and right. And in the end, you'll have the desires of your heart.

*Lord, take charge of my thought-life today, I pray.
I want beautiful thoughts! Amen.*

Date:

DEAR GOD, ...
....
....
....

I'm thankful for. . . ..
....
....
....
....
....
....
....

My worries. . . ..
....
....
....
....
....
....

People I am praying for. . . ..
....
....
....
....
....

Here's what's going on in my life. . .

MY NEEDS. . .

Other stuff I need to share with You, God. . .

AMEN.
Thank You, Father,
for hearing my prayers.

WEEK 18
Here Am I. . . Send Me!

Then I heard the voice of the Lord, saying, "Whom should I send? Who will go for Us?" Then I said, "Here am I. Send me!"
ISAIAH 6:8 NLV

Maybe you're one of those girls who strongly feels the call of God on her life. Maybe you've got big plans to go on a mission trip or to work with inner-city children. You don't worry about how uncomfortable things might get or how much it would cost. You're sure God will work all of that out.

Welcome to the ministry, girl! The truth is, the Lord has called all of us to spread the Good News. He's excited that you're excited about doing that, no matter how you choose to do it or where you decide to go. You might travel five miles or you might travel five thousand, but getting out of your comfort zone will be the best thing that ever happened to you. Sharing the Gospel message and the love of Christ with people who need to know Him is one of the greatest privileges in the world.

So buckle up, buttercup! Oh, the places you'll go with your hand in His.

Lord, I can hardly wait to see where You're taking me. Here am I. . .send me! Amen.

Send Me to the People

First of all, I ask you to pray much for
all men and to give thanks for them.
1 TIMOTHY 2:1 NLV

Have you ever met someone who's a "people person"? You know those people right away because they're totally comfortable, whether they're in a big crowd or in a small group. They always just seem to know what to say to put people at ease and to make them feel special.

Maybe you're a people person. And when you think about doing missions work, maybe the thing that gets you most excited isn't the program or the travel. . .it's the people you'll meet and the lives you'll impact. In fact, you can hardly wait to get there.

Sure, there might be some language barriers. And yes, there will be cultural differences. But you don't care about any of that. You just want to be where the people are—loving on them, sharing Jesus with them, and making sure their needs are met.

God loves people persons like you. They make everything so much fun.

Lord, I can hardly wait to hang out with those little kids
I'll meet on my next adventure. How fun it's going to be!

Send Me to Those in Need of a Friend

*So comfort each other and make each
other strong as you are already doing.*
1 THESSALONIANS 5:11 NLV

It doesn't matter what continent you live on or your economic status. You can be lonely, even if you live in a mansion on a tropical island.

When you think about all the people you'll meet in this life, are you most drawn to those who truly need a friend or to those who are already surrounded by people they adore? (Maybe both, right?)

Here's a nugget of truth: those people who are friendless really need you. And you don't have to travel to a different country to meet them. They're right there—in your science class, sitting alone at the lunch table, walking into the store completely alone. They need you. . .and in a strange way, you need them too. You won't feel whole until you've shared the love of Jesus with them.

So what's keeping you? Get over there and be a friend to the friendless!

*Lord, help me to get over any shyness as
I approach someone in need of a friend. Amen.*

Send Me to the Messy People

Preach the word; be ready in season and out of season; reprove,
rebuke, and exhort, with complete patience and teaching.
2 TIMOTHY 4:2 ESV

This world is filled with happy, healthy people, but if you look just below the surface, you'll see that many of them are just faking it. They're not as happy or as healthy as they appear. In fact, most people if they really came clean would have to say, "Yeah, I'm a hot mess under this facade."

You can relate because you're a hot mess too! So how good is God to introduce you to other hot messes?

When you connect with people who are just as flawed as you, you can relax a little because you're not out to impress them with your good works. You're just. . .you. And when they see how genuine you are, they can relax and be themselves too.

Messed-up people are worth it. They might not get fixed overnight, but when all is said and done, you'll be glad God connected you.

Lord, send me to the hot messes. I want to feel right at home! Amen.

Send Me to the World

And he said to them, "Go into all the world and
proclaim the gospel to the whole creation."
MARK 16:15 ESV

We're commanded in scripture to go into all the world to preach the Gospel. Where you end up—whether it's in your hometown or far, far away, there will be plenty of opportunities to tell people about Jesus.

There are 7.9 billion people on the planet right now. (Whoa. That's a lot.) You're just one person, and of those 7.9 billion, 2.5 billion are Christians. Stop to think about that for a moment. About one-third of the earth's population claims to know Christ.

Of course, this means that two-thirds do not know Him. But they can, and it's so simple! If each one would reach one, then another 2.5 billion would be won to the Lord. That would bring the number of Christians up to 5 billion. And if each one of those would reach one. . .well, you get the idea.

It's not as complicated as we've made it out to be. Each one simply needs to reach one.

Show me who I can reach, Lord. Amen.

Send Me to My Knees

The Lord is near to all who call on Him,
to all who call on Him in truth.
PSALM 145:18 NLV

Of all the places God wants to send you, this is the most important: He wants to send you. . .to your knees.

Yes, you read that right. He wants you to bow your knee to Him (symbolically and often physically), to commit yourself fully, completely, wholly to His way, His plan, and His great love. Before you can reach the world, your heart has to be fully prepared, after all.

To bow your knee to Christ is similar to what a king's subjects do as they enter his chamber. It's a sign of reverence and awe, an act of obedience and respect. So hit those knees, girl! Get your heart right with God, and then listen for His still, small voice so He can tell you what's coming next on your journey. One thing's for sure. . .as you commit yourself to Him, you're preparing yourself for an amazing adventure ahead!

Lord, today I submit myself to You. I come to You—my King
of kings and Lord of lords—and bow my knee as a sign of
my great love for You. Use me as You will, Lord. Amen.

Date:

DEAR GOD, ...
....
....
....

I'm thankful for. . . ..
....
....
....
....
....
....

My worries. . . ..
....
....
....
....
....

$

People I am praying for. . . ..
....
....
....
....

Here's what's going on in my life. . .

MY NEEDS. . .

Other stuff I need to share with You, God. . .

AMEN.
Thank You, Father, for hearing my prayers.

WEEK 19

You've Got Big Plans for Me!

For I know the plans I have for you, declares the LORD,
plans for welfare and not for evil, to give you a future and a hope.
JEREMIAH 29:11 ESV

Do you ever compare your life with the lives of those around you? Maybe your friends are uber-talented and super smart. It's easy to imagine them going to a fancy college or living the dream life, based on their own abilities. Then you examine your own and, at least to your way of thinking, you fall short. Very, very short. (Ugh! Comparison games are awful!)

Here's some good news: God isn't depending on your abilities. He will promote those He chooses to promote, regardless of their limitations. And He has big plans for you. Probably a lot bigger than you could ask or think.

So, brace yourself, girl! Get ready for the great reveal. The Lord is going to take you on a wonderful adventure. Just hang on for the ride.

Lord, I don't know where I'm going to go in this life, but I know
one thing—I can totally trust You because You're creative
and good. I can't wait to see where You're taking me! Amen.

Stir Up the Gifts

This is why I remind you to keep using the gift God gave you when I laid my hands on you. Now let it grow, as a small flame grows into a fire.
2 TIMOTHY 1:6 NCV

Don't you love this scripture? Paul encouraged Timothy to keep using the gift that was within him. Some versions use the phrase "stir up the gift." When you read those words do you think about a big soup pot with a spoon or a ladle in it?

Your gifts, talents, abilities, and God-given attributes, are like the ingredients of that soup. Every now and again you have to give them a good stir so that they rise to the top. And once they're visible, you use them. . .then use them again until they're fully developed.

Maybe you are a singer who aspires to be a worship leader. Or perhaps you're a dancer. Or maybe you are in gifted-and-talented classes at school and can see yourself one day teaching at a university. Begin to stir up the gifts now that will be necessary to make those dreams come true. Then watch as God adds His power to the mix. Wow! Those gifts are really going to take you far.

Lord, I will stir up the gift that You've placed inside of me.
I won't neglect it. I'll keep using and developing it until
I'm ready to do all You've called me to do. Amen.

Point Me in the Right Direction

*Trust in the LORD with all your heart, and do not lean on your
own understanding. In all your ways acknowledge him,
and he will make straight your paths.*
PROVERBS 3:5–6 ESV

Have you ever come to a fork in the road? You stand there, gazing to the right and then the left, to the right and then the left, but you're not sure which direction is the right one to take.

The truth is, there will be many fork-in-the-road experiences in your life. The only way you can settle the issue of which direction to go is by following the Lord and listening for His still, small voice. When you're standing at a fork in the road, He's whispering in your ear, "Turn to the right," or, "Turn to the left!" He's not going to leave you standing there, stranded and confused.

If you are at a fork in the road right now, simply pray and ask for God's guidance. He will surely give it so that you can step out in faith toward the great plans that He has for your life.

*I can't see what's coming around the next bend, but I know
I can trust You, Lord! You've got everything mapped out
in advance. All I need to do is listen and obey. Amen.*

Submitting to Your Will and Your Way

These all agreed as they prayed together. The women and
Mary the mother of Jesus and His brothers were there.
ACTS 1:14 NLV

Let's face it, we all want our own way. We're conditioned from the time we are toddlers to say, "Mine! Mine!" Rarely will you hear a toddler say, "I want to do it *your* way, Mommy, not my own." Truth be told, he wants to do it his way, and his way alone—one hundred percent of the time.

The problem is, many of us grow up but still have that same attitude. We don't want to submit to God's way. We want what we want. . .and that's it. There's no meeting in the middle or bending of the will.

For some people, anyway. But you? You're learning, aren't you? Sometimes the only way to get what you want is to submit to what you really need. And then you discover that what you *needed* is actually better than what you *wanted* in the first place.

Are you ready to submit to His perfect will today?

Lord, it's not always easy to submit, but that's what
I choose to do today. Have Your way, Lord. Amen.

On a Learning Curve

Let the wise hear and increase in learning,
and the one who understands obtain guidance.
PROVERBS 1:5 ESV

Picture a pianist on a stage playing a fabulous, complicated piece without any music in front of him. His fingers move with ease up and down the keyboard. He doesn't even seem nervous as he plays. Now imagine the years of practice that it took to get him to that point. He didn't just start yesterday.

The same is true with pro ball players. They don't just start out in T-ball and then end up with a million-dollar contract with a sports team. They work their way up the ladder and they practice, practice, practice.

Maybe you don't like that word *practice*. Maybe you would rather not sit for hours and play your clarinet or work on your vocal skills. But here's the truth: good things come to those who practice. Sure, there are a few naturally talented people out there who don't have to work as hard, but the majority of all gifted people have to work just as hard as you.

The payoff is terrific for those who stick with it. Are you going to be a girl who does?

Lord, I've got a stick-to-it attitude. Don't let me quit! Amen.

Helping Others Learn

Do not neglect to do good and to share what you have,
for such sacrifices are pleasing to God.
HEBREWS 13:16 ESV

God has called you to help others grow into who they're supposed to become. Of course, He wants to see you stir up the gifts that are inside your own life, but He's also interested in seeing you help develop the gifts in the lives of those around you.

That girl who wants to sing the solo in the church choir? If she's not quite there yet, why not work with her until she is? That young man who is particularly talented with drama? Encourage him to try out for the school play, then go see him when he gets a role.

There are lots of things you can do to stir up the gifts of those around you. Don't be so distracted by your own that you forget to build up others. You could be a gift-stirrer, girl! And who knows. . .the person you're encouraging might just change the world.

Show me who to encourage today, Lord.
Help me lift up a true world-changer, I pray. Amen.

Date

DEAR GOD, ...
....
....
....

I'm thankful for. . . ..
....
....
....
....
....
....
....

My worries. . . ..
....
....
....
....
....
....

People I am praying for. . . ..
....
....
....
....

Here's what's going on in my life. . .

MY NEEDS. . .

Other stuff I need to share
with You, God. . .

AMEN.
Thank You, Father,
for hearing my prayers.

WEEK 20

Your Kingdom Come

May Your holy nation come. What You want done,
may it be done on earth as it is in heaven.
MATTHEW 6:10 NLV

- -

"On earth as it is in heaven." Think about those words for a minute. Chances are pretty good you can't even imagine how glorious heaven is going to be, but this much you do know: it's not too early to start praying for a heavenly outcome right here, right now, while you're still on earth.

As you pray for that sick friend, pray, "On earth as it is in heaven." Hint: there's no sickness in heaven. As you pray for your parents' financial woes, pray, "On earth as it is in heaven." Hint: there's no financial lack in heaven.

You get the point. Everything in heaven is going to be, well, heavenly. God wants you to get used to the idea that you can start praying for a heavenly outcome now. There's no reason to wait, girl! Ready, set. . .pray.

- -

Lord, I get it. I don't have to wait. I can anticipate a heavenly outcome—
right here and right now. Thank You, Father! Amen.

Your Kingdom Come in My Heart

"Our Father in heaven, hallowed be your name. Your kingdom come,
your will be done, on earth as it is in heaven."
MATTHEW 6:9–10 ESV

Have you ever wondered what Jesus meant when He told us to pray that His kingdom would come? Was He talking about His literal kingdom? Is heaven going to invade our daily lives and set up camp in our living room? (That would be cool, actually.)

In heaven there is total kingdom rule. This means that God is fully in charge and no one is trying to force His hand or tell Him what to do. When you pray, "Your kingdom come, Lord," what you're really saying is, "Your way, not mine, Jesus."

That's easier said than done, isn't it? But when the kingdom of heaven invades your heart, it's even better than landing in your living room. Because real and lasting changes can take place inside that heart, and they will impact the world around you. So go ahead and pray it today: "Your kingdom come in my heart, Lord." Then step back and watch as God shows up and shows off.

Lord, I ask for that very thing today—may Your kingdom
come in my heart. Have Your way in me, I pray. Amen.

Your Kingdom Come in My Attitude

Have this mind among yourselves, which is yours in Christ Jesus.
PHILIPPIANS 2:5 ESV

Admit it: your attitude is not always the best. There are times when you fly off the handle and then regret the things you said and did. There are other times when you get a little too sarcastic with your mom or you snap back at your dad too easily. You don't give them a chance to say what they want to say before you're biting back.

You don't want to be this way. You never intended to be this way. And thank goodness, there is a way out. You can pray: "Your kingdom come in my attitude, Lord!" That's a brave prayer because the moment you pray it, you're giving the Creator of the universe full permission to change that attitude.

And change it, He will! You might just be surprised at how He turns your heart around. How He calms your voice when you're speaking. How He puts a proverbial piece of tape on your mouth to keep you from smarting off or saying the wrong thing to the wrong person. They don't call the Holy Spirit your guide for no reason. He's there to lead and guide you—what you do, and what you say. Now trust Him with the process.

Thank You, Lord, for bringing Your kingdom into my attitude.

Your Kingdom Come in My Relationships

*Do not be unequally yoked with unbelievers. For what
partnership has righteousness with lawlessness?
Or what fellowship has light with darkness?*
2 Corinthians 6:14 esv

What would our relationships be like if God had His way in every single one? Issues between parents and kids would simply go away. Fights between best friends would be nonexistent. Arguments between siblings wouldn't be necessary.

If God's kingdom truly came in every relationship in your life, everything would change. That teacher at school, the one who annoys you? God would work that out. That girl in your fifth period class who won't leave you alone? The Lord would soften her heart. That parent who's angry at you over something you did days ago? He might just let that go, once and for all.

Maybe this is the right day to pray that prayer. "Thy kingdom come in my relationships, Lord." Every single one. Every single time. In every single way. Now, watch and see what He does!

*I really want that, Lord! Make all my relationships as
strong and healthy (in You!) as they can be. Amen.*

Your Kingdom Come in My Work

Let the favor of the Lord our God be upon us, and establish the work of our hands upon us; yes, establish the work of our hands!
PSALM 90:17 ESV

God wants you to work "heartily." That means He wants you to throw your heart into it. Oh, you know what it's like to trudge through it, completely uncommitted. But He wants a much deeper level of commitment than that!

So what kind of work, exactly? Well, start with your tasks around the house. From there, think about your schoolwork. After that, any job you might have—whether it's babysitting the neighbor's kids or working for a boss at a big company.

Throw yourself into your work with the same level of enthusiasm you threw yourself into planning that surprise birthday party for your best friend. (Remember how much fun that was?) Work can be just as fun. No, really. It's all about attitude. When you pray, "Your kingdom come in my work," that's exactly what you can expect!

I'm looking forward to my work being fun, Lord!
Your kingdom come, I pray. Amen.

Your Kingdom Come in My Health

Beloved, I pray that all may go well with you and that you may be in good health, as it goes well with your soul.

3 JOHN 1:2 ESV

Sometimes you get so busy that you forget to focus on taking care of yourself. You don't eat the right foods. You don't get enough sleep. You make poor decisions, like not taking good enough care of your teeth or your hair. These things might not seem like a big deal, but over time you'll pay a price for neglecting your body like that.

Maybe it's time to pray, "Your kingdom come in my health." When you pray like that, you're really saying, "God, I give you full permission to change my thinking—about what, when, and how much I eat. About how long I sleep. About when I work and when I play. About, well, everything." Because if you're being totally honest, you have to admit that your health is impacted by pretty much every area of your life.

You want a long, healthy life. It starts by making great decisions while you're young. Why not start today?

Lord, I pray for Your kingdom to come in my health. Have Your way, I pray. Amen.

DEAR GOD, ...

....

....

....

I'm thankful for. . . ..

....

....

....

....

....

....

....

My worries. . . ..

....

....

....

....

....

....

People I am praying for. . . ..

....

....

....

....

Here's what's going on in my life. . . ..

....

....

....

....

MY NEEDS. . .

....

....

....

....

....

....

....

....

....

....

....

....

....

Other stuff I need to share
with You, God. . .

....

....

....

....

....

....

....

....

....

AMEN.
Thank You, Father,
for hearing my prayers.

WEEK 21

You Give Me All I Need!

And my God will supply every need of yours
according to his riches in glory in Christ Jesus.
PHILIPPIANS 4:19 ESV

It's remarkable to think about the fact that God knows what you need. He knows what kind of food you enjoy, where you live, and what sort of education you'll need for the job that lies ahead. He knows your financial concerns, and your wishes, wants, and desires. And He cares about all of that.

Best of all, God is a need-meeter. There's not a problem your parents have ever faced that He did not solve. He saw the time they were about to lose the house and He provided income. He saw that time they were short on food and provided groceries. He sees. . .and He supplies. So why would you ever doubt Him? If He's come through for your family time and time again, He'll do it the next time too.

Put your trust in Him today. He will make provision, no doubt about it. In fact, He can't wait to surprise you with how He plans to do it!

I can trust You to meet my needs, Lord. I'm so grateful! Amen.

You Provide Financially

Give us the bread we need today.
MATTHEW 6:11 NLV

Have you ever wondered why God doesn't just dump money from the sky to pay for all of your needs at once? Why does He give you just what you need for right now and not what you'll need a week from now or even a month from now? Wouldn't it make more sense to dump it all out at once? Then you wouldn't have to go to Him again and again.

God is much wiser than you. He knows that you would probably spend it all when you received it. That could be one reason He chooses to meet needs as they come up. But He's also testing your faith. He wants you to learn from the times when He provided for you so next time you'll have more faith when you ask Him. You can say, "He's done it before. I know He'll do it again."

He will, of course. He will always make financial provision for you. You don't have to live in fear. God's got you covered, girl!

Lord, thank You for making provision for me. You give me my daily bread, and right here, right now, that's all I really need. Amen.

You Take Care of My Body

*All things were made through him, and without
him was not any thing made that was made.*
JOHN 1:3 ESV

God made all things. Everything. You might look at something like a car and say, "Well, He didn't make that." Oh, but didn't He? He created all the materials necessary to make it and gave humans the ingenuity to put those materials together. So in essence, He made the car.

God made you too. Every cell. Every hair. Every muscle. Every tendon. He knows your inner workings and your outer beauty. There's nothing about your body that He does not know. That's why you can trust Him with it, because He made it.

If your car broke down, who would you take it to? A specialist—most people take the car back to the dealership where they bought it because the people there know that car inside and out. So when something goes wrong with your body, go back to the specialist who designed it in the first place. You can trust Him with every fiber of your being.

*Lord, I have some concerns about my body. Is everything working like it
should? Thank You for taking care of me, inside and out. Amen.*

You Take Care of Those I Love

*"Look at the birds of the air: they neither sow nor reap
nor gather into barns, and yet your heavenly Father
feeds them. Are you not of more value than they?"*
MATTHEW 6:26 ESV

You might think that no one cares about your loved ones as much as you do, but you would be wrong. There's one who cares even more than you do! (Seems impossible, right?!) That time your mom was in a car accident? God was right there, taking care of her. That time your kid sister was admitted to the hospital with appendicitis? He was there too.

God cares for His kids. And here's a fun fact—He doesn't just care about the ones who have placed their trust in Him. He loves all people across the planet the same. So you can trust Him with the people in your world—your family, friends, classmates, and so on.

Think about today's verse: God cares about the birds of the air. He makes sure they have everything they need. They don't plant crops or plow the fields, and yet they have all the food they need. If God cares enough to tend to the birds of the air, how much more will He take care of the human beings He created?

*Lord, I can trust You with my loved ones (even the ones I've been so
worried about). Thank You for taking such great care of all of us. Amen.*

You Take Care of My Broken Heart

The LORD is far from the wicked,
but he hears the prayer of the righteous.
PROVERBS 15:29 ESV

Sometimes no one knows what's going on in your heart because you refuse to tell them. You don't want anyone to know the heartache or the pain you're experiencing. You think they wouldn't understand. Or maybe they might judge you.

God understands. And He's not judging your broken heart. He's tending to it, like a doctor would tend to an open wound. He's adding the antiseptic of His cleansing power, the ointment of His Holy Spirit, and the bandages paid for when His Son went to the cross and died for you.

God cares. And that broken heart? It might feel like it's going to last forever, but it won't. One day it will be a distant memory, just something that happened to you "back in the day."

The Lord hears your prayers—whether your heart is broken or whole. Today, why not trust Him to mend the broken places and make things right again?

Lord, I trust You with my heart. You created it,
so You must know it better than anyone, including me.
Thank You for caring about what I'm going through. Amen.

You Give Me Hope When I'm Hopeless

*For in this hope we were saved. Now hope that is seen
is not hope. For who hopes for what he sees? But if we
hope for what we do not see, we wait for it with patience.*
ROMANS 8:24–25 ESV

"Hope that is seen is not hope." What do you make of that line?

Here's the truth: it takes very little faith to hope for something that you can see with your own eyes or hear with your own ears. Example: When you were a kid, you hoped the ice-cream man would come by your house. You heard the music playing and your hope grew. He was getting close! Did it take a great amount of faith to believe he was coming? No, because the music convinced you.

But what if you hoped and hoped and never heard the music? Ah, that's when trust kicks in. There are things in this life that you hope for, but you never hear the music. You don't see anything happening with your eyes. But you keep on hoping, keep on believing, because that's what people of faith do. They don't give up, even when the song isn't playing.

*Lord, I will keep my hope and my trust in You, even when I can't see
with my eyes or hear with my ears. I can trust You, Father! Amen.*

Date:

DEAR GOD, ...
....
....
....

I'm thankful for. . . ..
....
....
....
....
....
....
....

My worries. . . ..
....
....
....
....
....
....

People I am praying for. . . ..
....
....
....
....
....

Here's what's going on in my life. . .

MY NEEDS. . .

Other stuff I need to share
with You, God. . .

AMEN.
Thank You, Father,
for hearing my prayers.

WEEK 22
Heaven Is Coming!

*But according to his promise we are waiting for new
heavens and a new earth in which righteousness dwells.*
2 PETER 3:13 ESV

Heaven is coming. Don't those words give you hope? When you're facing a terrible situation or feeling all alone: heaven is coming. When someone you love is about to pass away from a lengthy illness: heaven is coming. When the trials of life seem to never end: heaven is coming. And when we get there, all trials will be a thing of the past. All sickness will be over. All pain will cease. There will be no more heartache, no more tears, no more jealousy, no more anger.

Heaven will be. . .heavenly. Truly. For there, at the center of it all, will sit the One who loves you most and knows you best. You'll spend eternity in a completely different frame of mind than you spent your days on earth. Here, you worry and fret. There? Every need will be met.

Heaven is coming. The next time you're walking through a tough season, just remind yourself: This is a non-eternal situation. A better one is on the way.

*Lord, I'm so grateful for the promise of heaven.
I can't wait to see it with my own eyes! Amen.*

Heaven in My Heart

Instead, they were longing for a better country—a heavenly one.
Therefore God is not ashamed to be called their God,
for he has prepared a city for them.
HEBREWS 11:16 NIV

God has placed eternity in your heart. From the moment you gave your life to Jesus, He planted heaven—like a seed—in your heart. And you've been longing for it ever since, whether you realize it or not.

That desire inside of you for peace between your friends? That's a heavenly desire. That longing for the sick to be made whole? That's a heavenly longing. That feeling you have when you're in an amazing worship service, like God is right there, hugging you? That's a heavenly feeling, one you're going to experience for all eternity.

Yes, He placed heaven in your heart, and He wants you to share the promise of it with everyone you meet along life's journey. You might say, "Um, I can't do that." It might be easier than you think. Just live your life for Him, and when opportunities arise, when people say, "Why are you always smiling?" you can simply respond, "I've got a promise locked up in my heart." That's a great conversation starter!

Lord, thank You for placing heaven in my heart! Amen.

Heaven on Your Mind

The wall was made of jasper. The city was made of pure gold. This gold was as clear as glass. The city was built on every kind of stone that was worth much money. The first stone was jasper. The second was sapphire. The third was chalcedony. The fourth was emerald. The fifth was sardonyx. The sixth was sardius. The seventh was chrysolite. The eighth was beryl. The ninth was topaz. The tenth was chrysoprase. The eleventh was jacinth and the twelfth was amethyst. The twelve gates were twelve pearls. Each gate was made from one pearl. The street of the city was pure gold. It was as clear as glass.
REVELATION 21:18–21 NLV

When you read this description of heaven, no doubt your heart is racing. You can't even begin to imagine how beautiful it will be. How bright. How sparkling. How glorious. It will be better than any movie set or any book you've ever read. And it will be your home, not just for a few years (like the house you're living in now) but forever.

God planted this beautiful image in your mind so you would think about it whenever life gets hard. Instead of focusing your thoughts on the problem, focus on the solution—the Maker of heaven and earth!

*Lord, thank You for fixing my thoughts on heaven,
not on the things of this world. Amen.*

Heaven in My Perspective

This is life that lasts forever. It is to know You, the only true God, and to know Jesus Christ Whom You have sent.

JOHN 17:3 NLV

Have you ever heard someone say, "You need to change your perspective, girl!" They're asking you to change how you view things (the lens you see things through). Once you come to Christ, you're given a heavenly lens to view life through. Your whole perspective changes when you view troubles, joys, and even people through that special lens.

So what does it mean to have a heavenly perspective? For one thing, you don't get hung up on the things that happen here on earth, no matter how tragic or ugly. They're non-eternal. You don't worry so much about what people think about your physical body (how you look, how talented you are. . .or aren't) because that too is non-eternal. (You're getting a new body in heaven, FYI.)

God wants you to have an eternal perspective, one that sees every situation, every person, through the lens of heaven. That's a whole different way to live!

Lord, thank You for changing my perspective! I want to view life through the lens of heaven, Father! Amen.

Heaven in My Actions

But the fruit that comes from having the Holy Spirit in our lives is: love, joy, peace, not giving up, being kind, being good, having faith, being gentle, and being the boss over our own desires. The Law is not against these things.
GALATIANS 5:22–23 NLV

When you have an eternal perspective, it changes not just your thinking but your actions. Every decision you make is made in light of eternity. When you're seeing through the God-lens of heaven, your decisions are made with that end goal in mind. You want to take others with you. So that means you don't come out swinging when that girl in your math class cusses you out. You pray for her and you sincerely stand in the gap for her. Why? So that she will see your loving heart and want what you have. The end goal is to lead her to Christ by loving her into the Kingdom.

It's so simple, really. There's no need to complicate it. A heavenly perspective leads to heavenly actions—kindness, gentleness, self-control. All those fruits of the Spirit will cause others to view you differently.

Lord, I want to be a shining example of You, so that my friends and loved ones will come to know You too! Amen.

Telling Others about Heaven

Blessed are those who mourn, for they shall be comforted.
MATTHEW 5:4 ESV

Imagine you're at a funeral. The family of the deceased is deep in mourning and you don't blame them. The loss is severe. You wonder how they will ever get through it. Then the pastor begins to speak about heaven. . .about the new home their loved one has gone to. By the time he's done describing it, there are smiles on every face. The perspective of the family has changed—from mourning to joy. They still miss her, of course, but knowing she's gone to live in heaven brings such comfort.

It's so important to share the message of heaven with others so they can have hope as well. When you know where you're headed (or where your loved ones are headed), it makes the transition easier. Not easy. . .but easier.

Share the joy of heaven as often as you can. Bring hope to a sad, broken world.

Lord, I'm so excited about seeing my grandparents,
great-grandparents, and other friends and loved
ones when I get to heaven. What a day that will be!

Date:

DEAR GOD, _____
_____
_____
_____

I'm thankful for. . . _____
_____
_____
_____
_____
_____
_____
_____

My worries. . . _____
_____
_____
_____
_____
_____

People I am praying for. . . _____
_____
_____
_____
_____

Here's what's going on in my life. . .

MY NEEDS. . .

Other stuff I need to share with You, God. . .

AMEN.
Thank You, Father,
for hearing my prayers.

WEEK 23

Forgive Us Our Debts

"Forgive us our sins as we forgive those who sin against us."
MATTHEW 6:12 NLV

Have you ever owed anyone money? It's a horrible feeling, isn't it? Knowing you have a debt that needs to be paid can be a real pain, especially if you don't know how you're going to repay it.

Here's the deal: when it comes to God, you have a debt that cannot be paid. Your sin was separating you from Him. But then He sent His Son, Jesus, who paid the price for you. When He died on the cross, He took all your sins onto Himself and took care of them, once and for all. Wow! Why would He do that? Out of His great love for you, of course!

Now that you've been greatly forgiven, it's time to apply that same strategy to others. Some of your friends and loved ones have emotional debts they can't pay. You keep waiting for payback, but it's not coming. That apology your BFF needs to offer? She might not. But you can forgive her anyway. Don't wait until the apologies come. Let things go easily. After all, you've been forgiven much.

Lord, You've forgiven my sins. Now show me how to forgive others, I pray. Amen.

As We Forgive Others

*"If you forgive people their sins, your Father in heaven
will forgive your sins also. If you do not forgive people
their sins, your Father will not forgive your sins."*
MATTHEW 6:14–15 NLV

Take a close look at today's verse. It's really more of a command than a statement, isn't it? It's kind of scary to think that God will refuse to forgive us if we refuse to forgive others, but it's clearly stated in this scripture.

Why do you think He cares so much about whether you will—or won't—forgive someone else? After all, He knows the pain those people caused you. He should understand. . .right?

He does understand, even more than you do. Holding someone in unforgiveness doesn't just hurt them, it hurts you. It causes your heart to grow hard, and bitterness to take up residence inside you. It causes unnecessary separation and can even involve other friends or family members.

Forgive. It's God's way. After all, He forgave you for all the unmentionable things you did. The least you can do to honor His gift is to forgive others as well.

*Lord, this is a hard one. There are people I haven't been
ready to forgive. Help me let go today, I pray. Amen.*

I'm Having a Hard Time Forgiving Myself, Though...

*If we tell Him our sins, He is faithful and we can depend on Him
to forgive us of our sins. He will make our lives clean from all sin.*
1 JOHN 1:9 NLV

You've done some things in the past that no one knows about but you. Bad things. Things you wish you could change. And you've also done things that everyone knows about. You're embarrassed. Ashamed. Filled with regret. And you haven't been able to forgive yourself, as hard as you've tried.

Here's the truth, girl—everyone has stuff in the rearview mirror they wish they could get rid of. But you can't go backward and undo them. You can, however, confess them to God. When you do that, you can count on two things: (1) He will forgive you, right then and there. (2) He will show you how to move forward, which is really what you want and need.

Tell Him. He already knows anyway. But tell Him for your sake, so you can let go of it, once and for all.

Lord, there are some things I haven't forgiven myself for. Today I'm bringing those things to You so I can finally let go of the shame and regret. Amen.

Forgiving the Ones I Thought I Could Trust

Then Peter came up and said to him, "Lord, how often will my brother sin against me, and I forgive him? As many as seven times?" Jesus said to him, "I do not say to you seven times, but seventy times seven."

MATTHEW 18:21–22 ESV

You thought you could trust her. But this time? Man, she really let you down. She gossiped about you behind your back, sharing your struggles with other people who had no right to know. And then, to make things worse, she lied about it. Denied the whole thing.

Now what? You're sadder, but wiser. But how do you handle the situation with this friend? Drop her like a hot potato? Give her a piece of your mind? Tell others her flaws like she shared yours?

The answer to that question is none of the above. You have to start with forgiving her, even if she hasn't admitted the truth. If you begin to pray for her, if you can truly let go of what she's done to you even before she asks, then God can intervene and work on her heart. Before long, she's going to come clean and then the two of you can have a heart-to-heart. Does this mean you trust her with the juicy news next time? Maybe not. Only time will tell. But forgive her anyway.

Lord, this is a tough one, but today I choose to forgive _____.

Do I Have to Forgive Everyone?

*"When you stand to pray, if you have anything against anyone,
forgive him. Then your Father in heaven will forgive your sins also."*
MARK 11:25 NLV

You know how it is. . .you're about ready to pray but your mind keeps wandering. You can't stop thinking about what that group of girls said about you, how they hurt you. Ugh. It's really hard to focus on God when you're still mad and upset about what they did. And then you read a verse like this one: "If you have anything against anyone, forgive him." Really, Lord? You have to forgive everyone?

It's tempting to hang on to unforgiveness toward one or two people—the ones who've really, truly hurt you. You justify it with words like, "Yeah, well, you have no idea what they did to me."

Now imagine if Jesus used those words about you. Imagine He went to His Father and said, "Dad, I would forgive that one, but You have no idea what she did to me!" Kind of puts things in perspective. When Jesus forgave, He forgave everyone. And—even though it seems impossible at times—He wants the same response from you.

*Okay, Lord. . .here goes. The list is going to be long,
but I choose to forgive _____.*

A Forgiveness Lifestyle

*"Judge not, and you will not be judged; condemn not, and you
will not be condemned; forgive, and you will be forgiven."*
LUKE 6:37 ESV

You know how the smell of popcorn at the movie theater makes you want to eat it—and the sooner, the better? You weren't even thinking about popcorn before you arrived, but now it's all you can think of! There's a magnetic pull, tugging you toward the concession stand. You'll never make it through the movie if you don't get some popcorn! You can almost taste it now—that hot, salty yumminess!

That "tug" to get popcorn might seem like a silly example, but that's kind of how God wants you to live when it comes to forgiving others. He wants the scent of forgiveness to be so powerful in your life that you have to forgive. You simply can't move forward until you do.

Forgiveness is like a bucket of hot, salty, buttery popcorn, ready to be shared with all of those who've hurt you. Once you start spreading it around, everyone has to have a bite!

*Lord, today I ask for an invasion of forgiveness to flood my soul. May it
become a lifestyle choice, Lord. . .something that comes so naturally
that others want to dip their hands in the bucket too. Amen.*

Date:

DEAR GOD,
_____
_____
_____
_____

I'm thankful for. . .
_____
_____
_____
_____
_____
_____
_____

My worries. . .
_____
_____
_____
_____
_____
_____

People I am praying for. . .
_____
_____
_____
_____
_____

Here's what's going on in my life. . . ..
....
....
....
....

MY NEEDS. . .

....
....
....
....
....
....
....
....
....
....
....
....
....
....
....

Other stuff I need to share
with You, God. . .

....
....
....
....
....
....
....
....

AMEN.
Thank You, Father,
for hearing my prayers.

WEEK 24

This Stinks!

Declare me innocent, O God! Defend me against these ungodly people. Rescue me from these unjust liars.

You've been falsely accused. Now all of your peers actually think you did it. . .only you didn't. Nothing you say seems to convince them. Their minds are made up. And you? You're wishing you could crawl into a hole somewhere. Why won't anyone come to your defense?

Situations like these really stink! They're not fair. But you don't have to give up when you've been falsely accused. God is your defender, and He has a way of bringing the truth to light. So hang in there. Hold fast to your faith. Don't stop praying. Don't stop believing. Don't stop speaking truth. But be patient because God has to work this out on His timetable. He will defend you against the ungodly. He will rescue you from liars.

Watch and see.

Lord, my heart feels like it's all twisted up inside me. I hate how this feels! I don't like it when the crowd is against me. Please defend me, Lord! Come to my rescue, and shed light on this situation so that everyone will see the truth. Amen.

School Stinks!

It is senseless to pay to educate a fool,
since he has no heart for learning.
PROVERBS 17:16 NLT

It's been a rough season for you academically. Tests. Projects. Homework. Teachers in a bad mood. You can't seem to do anything right, and you're wondering if it's going to go on like this forever.

Thank goodness most of these seasons are just that. . .seasons. They don't last forever. You move on to other classes, other teachers. You make it through that one course you're sure you'll fail. Somehow things come together. But that doesn't make you feel better in the moment, does it?

Today, if you're struggling with school-related woes, don't forget to mention them to God. He wants you to bring those problems to Him. He knows how to open your heart and mind so that you better understand the assignments. He knows how to adjust your calendar to make more time for the work. And He even knows how to touch the heart of that teacher, the one who's always so grumpy. In other words, He can handle this. So take your hands off, girl. Give it to God and watch Him work.

I trust You with these issues, God! Amen.

People Stink!

Love must be sincere. Hate what is evil; cling to what is good.
Be devoted to one another in love. Honor one another above yourselves.
ROMANS 12:9–10 NIV

People are hard. Sometimes they're ridiculously hard. And some are tougher than others. In fact, they seem to thrive on making life difficult for everyone around them. But. . .why? Who gets their kicks making others miserable?

On days like this, when you're done peopling, it might be a good idea to pull away and have some alone time. Get by yourself and listen to some music or grab one of those grown-up coloring books and get some of your angst out on paper. Then, when your heart has settled a little, pour out your people troubles to God. He sees all and knows all anyway, but He loves it when you actually share what you're thinking and feeling.

By the way, you're a people too. And it's possible (just imagine this) that someone somewhere is escaping to their quiet space to get away from you too. (Hey, it could happen!) People are people. They aren't easy. But they're totally and completely worth it.

Lord, thanks for showing me how to "people."
I want to get better at it! Amen.

My Attitude Stinks!

*Know this, my beloved brothers: let every person be quick
to hear, slow to speak, slow to anger; for the anger of
man does not produce the righteousness of God.*
JAMES 1:19–20 ESV

Some days you just have a stinky attitude. It's like you wake up with it or something. And you can't seem to shake it, no matter what happens. Every little thing is a trigger, setting you off. You don't mean to snap at people, but it's almost like it's out of your control.

On days like that, you have to acknowledge that you do have the power to control your reactions. You can't use excuses like, "This day stinks." Maybe it does stink, but you don't have to. You can calm yourself. You can take a deep breath, count to ten, and deal with things differently. You're not a ticking time bomb, waiting to blow up.

Take a close look at today's scripture: "be quick to hear, slow to speak, slow to anger." Notice the time references there? Instead of quick reactions and responses, you need to be quick only to hear, not to act. Your responses, especially on hard days, need to be s-l-o-w.

*Lord, I want to slow down my reactions so this day doesn't
get totally out of hand, but I need Your help! Amen.*

This Situation Stinks!

*Blessed is the one who perseveres under trial because,
having stood the test, that person will receive the crown
of life that the Lord has promised to those who love him.*
JAMES 1:12 NIV

What does it mean to persevere under trial? It means you don't give up, even when you feel like it. Even when others would totally throw in the towel.

You were kind of hoping there wouldn't be any trials in your life, right? Those unfair situations? Let them happen to other people, not you. But here's the thing about life—it rains on the just and the unjust. Bad things sometimes happen to good people. And unfair situations—even totally stinky ones—crop up from time to time. It's how you deal with them that matters. If you say you're a Christian, then you'd better act like one, even if everything around you is swirling like a powerful tornado.

So persevere under the trials, girl. They will come and go, but your resilient spirit will be a testament to your faith that no one can question.

*Lord, I will keep standing, keep believing, and keep hoping.
I won't give up, even in stinky situations! Amen.*

Getting Over the Stench

Brothers and sisters, I do not consider myself yet to have taken hold of it. But one thing I do: Forgetting what is behind and straining toward what is ahead, I press on toward the goal to win the prize for which God has called me heavenward in Christ Jesus.
PHILIPPIANS 3:13–14 NIV

That last trauma you faced was a doozie. You almost didn't make it through. But you did make it, and now you're on the other side. Just one problem. . . the pain of that trauma is still with you. It's still wearing you down and causing after effects.

Think about a mother who just gave birth. She's still in pain for a few days after the baby arrives. Her body is adjusting. But looking into the face of that baby makes it all worth it. The same is true with what you've been through. It was painful. But now that you've come through it, the joy of what's in front of you is better than—bigger than—the lingering pain.

You'll get past this. No, really. At some point in the future the ickiness will be nothing but a distant memory. And you'll be so glad you kept going. The lingering pain will fade away and you'll be back to normal in no time.

Lord, thank You for allowing me to move on. I don't want to get hung up in the problems—or the pain—of yesterday. Amen.

Date:

DEAR GOD,
_____
_____
_____
_____

I'm thankful for. . .
_____
_____
_____
_____
_____
_____
_____

My worries. . .
_____
_____
_____
_____
_____
_____

People I am praying for. . .
_____
_____
_____
_____
_____

Here's what's going on in my life. . .

MY NEEDS. . .

Other stuff I need to share with You, God. . .

AMEN.
Thank You, Father,
for hearing my prayers.

WEEK 25
Do You Still Heal?

He himself bore our sins in his body on the tree, that we might die to sin and live to righteousness. By his wounds you have been healed.

1 PETER 2:24 ESV

You often wonder if God still heals like He did in the olden days. Sometimes your loved ones get sick and don't seem to get better. Some have even passed away. Is this all part of God's plan—sickness and suffering?

Here's a sobering truth—with the fall of Adam and Eve in the Garden of Eden, sin entered the world. And when it entered, it brought with it sickness and death (two things that were never part of God's original plan). There will be ultimate healing when we all get to heaven. We know this for sure because the Bible tells us there's no pain or sorrow there. But until then, continue to pray in faith for those who are sick.

God is still in the healing business. It doesn't always look like you imagine—sometimes He heals by taking someone on to heaven so they can enjoy a totally healthy environment. But remember, when Jesus died on the cross, His wounds were meant to bring healing—to our souls, our hearts, and our bodies.

*Lord, I don't always know how healing will play out,
but I trust You with my loved ones. Bring healing in
Your own time and Your own way, I pray. Amen.*

Heal This Heart

He heals the brokenhearted and binds up their wounds.
PSALM 147:3 ESV

Have you ever met someone who was heartsick? You could tell by being around her that her heavy heart was ruling every emotion, every situation, every relationship. It's hard to be around someone who's always sad, isn't it? You don't know what to say, except, "I'm so sorry," and "I'm praying for you." Mostly you just wish they could put the pain behind them and move on.

Human beings were never meant to live forever with broken, wounded hearts. Jesus came to bring healing—to hearts, minds, and bodies. So there's no reason to allow your heart to linger in pain for long when the solution is to place it in His hands.

Today, if your heart is aching or breaking, give it to Jesus. Picture yourself physically handing it over into His tender hands. Then imagine He reshapes and reworks your heart, breathing new life into it, a life free from agony and despair.

Let it go, girl. It's more than just a song. Let it go. Give it to Him. Be set free from the pain today.

Lord, today I give this broken heart to You. Mend it, I pray. Amen.

Heal This Relationship

*Above all, keep loving one another earnestly
since love covers a multitude of sins.*
1 PETER 4:8 ESV

Is there a lost or broken relationship that you're grieving? You might think it's completely over, but God has a way of surprising you. People reconnect after months—or years—apart. They forgive each other. They get over it. They move on.

Think of the people you've separated from. Some of those separations were meant to be. (Hey, some folks can be toxic and you need to avoid them.) Others, though? It's kind of sad to push that friendship aside because it was a really good one.

This would be a good time to pray about relationships like that. They might appear broken now, but maybe they won't be broken forever. Ask God to show you which friends to reconnect with and which ones to avoid. He'll show you, if you put your trust in Him.

*Lord, I want to be careful not to go back into any codependent
relationships, but I also want to be open to the possibility of
reconciling with others I've lost touch with. Lead me, I pray. Amen.*

Heal the One I Love

Is anyone among you suffering? He should pray. Is anyone happy? He should sing songs of thanks to God. Is anyone among you sick? He should send for the church leaders and they should pray for him. They should pour oil on him in the name of the Lord. The prayer given in faith will heal the sick man, and the Lord will raise him up. If he has sinned, he will be forgiven.
JAMES 5:13–15 NLV

You can't help but worry about your loved ones who are sick. And when you're super close to them—say, a parent or a best friend, it can be even tougher to watch them suffer. (Hey, it's awful to watch a loved one go through pain! You wish you could take it for them.)

You can and should pray for the one in pain, of course. But think about this—God, your heavenly Father, watches you go through pain too. It breaks His heart. As much as you care about your family member who's sick, He cares about you when you're hurting. And He wants to see you healed as much as you want to see your loved one healed.

How wonderful to be loved like that!

Lord, I'm so glad You care. Thank You for giving me that same caring heart to love others. Amen.

Heal the Secret Places

"For God can do all things."
LUKE 1:37 NLV

Your friend is struggling. She won't tell you what's going on, but she's definitely going through something tough. You wish you knew how to pray, but you don't. All you can say is, "Lord, please fix whatever is upsetting her."

And sometimes a prayer like that is enough. Because God sees what's really going on. He doesn't need to be told what she's struggling with. His eyes are already on the problem, and He's hard at work on her behalf, mending the broken places.

Aren't you glad you serve a God who sees into the secret chambers of the heart? Aren't you relieved that He knows, even when we don't? And isn't it miraculous that He created that heart in the first place and is the best One to tend to it?

He heals the secret places—in your friend's heart and in yours too. So if you're battling secret issues today, let Him sweep in and take care of them. You'll be better in no time.

Lord, thank You for healing the secret places! You can do all things, even fixing the things I can't see. I'm so grateful! Amen.

Heal This Broken Planet

And God said, "Let the waters under the heavens be gathered together into one place, and let the dry land appear." And it was so.
GENESIS 1:9 ESV

Planet Earth is always dealing with struggles. Earthquakes. Tornadoes. Climate issues. The effects of littering and carbon emissions. There will always be problems due to humans not taking care of it properly, but there are also groanings that have nothing to do with us. The earth, after all, is aging rapidly. We're not meant to live here forever. (It's not like heaven, which is built for eternity.)

Across the globe there are other heartaches as well—poverty, sickness, sex trafficking, and prostitution. These are overwhelming issues, for sure, and not all of those issues will be solved in your lifetime. But you can pray about any and all of it. Pray for the people across the globe dealing with the effects of poverty. Pray for those who face religious persecution. Pray for the ones who have had their innocence stolen from them. And pray that people in every home in every city in every country on every continent would come to know Christ. Only then will true healing come.

*Lord, I pray for this beautiful planet You
created and all that are on it. Amen.*

Date:

DEAR GOD, ...
....
....
....

I'm thankful for. . . ..
....
....
....
....
....
....
....

My worries. . . ..
....
....
....
....
....
....

People I am praying for. . . ..
....
....
....
....

Here's what's going on in my life. . .

MY NEEDS. . .

Other stuff I need to share
with You, God. . .

AMEN.
Thank You, Father,
for hearing my prayers.

WEEK 26
A Fruity Life

But the fruit that comes from having the Holy Spirit in our lives is: love, joy, peace, not giving up, being kind, being good, having faith, being gentle, and being the boss over our own desires. The Law is not against these things.

GALATIANS 5:22–23 NLV

How sad would it be, to walk into an orchard during harvest season and find the trees withered and barren? No apples on the apple trees. No cherries on the cherry trees. No oranges on the orange trees. What a lot of wasted potential, right? Those trees were meant to bear fruit. Otherwise, what good are they?

The same can be said about you. You were meant to bear fruit—love, joy, peace, perseverance, kindness, goodness, faithfulness, gentleness, and self-control. When you don't exhibit those things, you're like a withered fruit tree in a fruitless orchard. Your potential is lost. Others don't benefit. (Hey, think about it—when you're not exhibiting love, kindness, and so on, people really don't get much benefit from your life.)

You were meant to blossom and flourish, girl! So keep that fruit healthy. Be productive. Make it count!

Lord, I want to bear good fruit. Keep me alive and healthy, I pray. Amen.

Love, a Lovely Fruit

*If I speak with human eloquence and angelic ecstasy but
don't love, I'm nothing but the creaking of a rusty gate. If I speak
God's Word with power, revealing all his mysteries and making
everything plain as day, and if I have faith that says to a mountain,
"Jump," and it jumps, but I don't love, I'm nothing.*
1 CORINTHIANS 13:1–2 MSG

Of all the fruits in the spiritual fruit bowl, there's one you simply can't do without—love. Without love, nothing is possible. In fact, if you try to live without love, you'll fail every time.

So what does a love-life look like? *"Love never gives up. Love cares more for others than for self. Love doesn't want what it doesn't have. Love doesn't strut, doesn't have a swelled head, doesn't force itself on others, isn't always 'me first,' doesn't fly off the handle, doesn't keep score of the sins of others, doesn't revel when others grovel, takes pleasure in the flowering of truth, puts up with anything, trusts God always, always looks for the best, never looks back, but keeps going to the end"* (1 Corinthians 13: 4–7 MSG).

Love never gives up. Never, ever, ever.

Lord, may I always show love! Amen.

Joy, Can't Do without It!

*Be full of joy always because you belong
to the Lord. Again I say, be full of joy!*
PHILIPPIANS 4:4 NLV

Jolly joy! Where would we be without it? Some girls just seem to radiate this fruit of the Spirit. They're all smiles, the life of the party, the happy-go-lucky ones. You, on the other hand? You have to work a little harder to be joyful at times. It's not that you don't want to. It's just that you get bogged down by the cares of life.

That's why prayer is so important. The enemy of your soul wants nothing more than to rob you of your joy. But you won't let him, will you? Nope! Ain't gonna happen. You'll spend time in prayer asking God to restore the joy of your salvation so you're freed up to share the Gospel message with hope and positivity.

God is good. He brings joy in the middle of sorrow. And, if you pray, He will show you how to keep your joy, no matter what you're going through.

*Lord, I don't ever want to lose my joy.
Infuse me with more of it today, I pray. Amen.*

Peace Like a Soft Blanket

Do not worry. Learn to pray about everything. Give thanks
to God as you ask Him for what you need. The peace of
God is much greater than the human mind can understand.
This peace will keep your hearts and minds through Christ Jesus.
PHILIPPIANS 4:6–7 NLV

Peace is a heavenly gift. It's that warm, cozy blanket that wraps you and makes things comfortable. But peace is also a weapon. The Bible says that you need to strap on the shoes of peace every day. In other words, you can walk in total peace, above the circumstances in your life.

Example: Your parents are going through a rough patch. They're ready to call it quits on the marriage. Mom is in turmoil over where you will live, how the financial stuff will work. . .all of it. You could give in to fear, but you decide not to. Instead, you pray for peace.

And God gives it! For some supernatural reason, you're not afraid. You use that peace as a weapon against fear, against doubt, and against despair. And, in the end, when your parents decide to give the marriage one last try, you're glad you kept yourself cloaked in God's supernatural peace!

Lord, thank You for that warm, cozy blanket of peace! Amen.

Gentleness: Not Always Easy!

"Take my yoke upon you, and learn from me, for I am gentle and lowly in heart, and you will find rest for your souls."

MATTHEW 11:29 ESV

Whoa, girl! Easy there! Maybe you heard those words growing up. Maybe you were rough. Careless. You broke Mom's favorite lamp or knocked pictures off the wall when playing too rough with your siblings. And your parents clucked their tongues and said, "Calm down, girl! Be gentle!"

Gentleness doesn't come easily to some of us, that's a fact. We have to work hard at it. It's especially hard when you're in a tough situation and someone has come out swinging against you. You want to swing back. But God has given you gentleness as a weapon. It's far more effective than giving your opponent a black eye, and it throws them off every single time. When you respond with gentleness, you diffuse the situation.

Today, pray that God will give you His gentleness so you can win the battles you face.

Lord, thank You for making me gentle like You.
I need more of this gift in my life!

Self-Controls: Can We Talk about This One?

But remember this—the wrong desires that come into your life aren't anything new and different. Many others have faced exactly the same problems before you. And no temptation is irresistible. You can trust God to keep the temptation from becoming so strong that you can't stand up against it, for he has promised this and will do what he says. He will show you how to escape temptation's power so that you can bear up patiently against it.

1 CORINTHIANS 10:13 TLB

That piece of cake is staring you in the face. You want it. You have to have it. Your mouth is watering as you imagine how amazing it's going to taste. But then again, you promised yourself you would cut back on sweets, and this time you really meant it!

Oh, but it's calling your name! That rich chocolate icing. It's teasing and tempting you and you're about to cave! Only you don't. Because you're reminded of this verse—that nothing is irresistible. You can (truly!) trust God to keep the temptations from being too strong. Whew! Isn't that a relief? Pray about it, girl. Give it to Jesus. Then thank Him for giving you the strength to say no.

Today I'm saying no to temptation, Lord!

Date

DEAR GOD, ...
....
....
....

I'm thankful for. . . ..
....
....
....
....
....
....
....

My worries. . . ..
....
....
....
....
....
....

People I am praying for. . . ..
....
....
....
....
....

Here's what's going on in my life. . .

MY NEEDS. . .

Other stuff I need to share
with You, God. . .

AMEN.
Thank You, Father,
for hearing my prayers.

WEEK 27

Weapons for War! (Armed and Ready)

For we do not wrestle against flesh and blood, but against the rulers, against the authorities, against the cosmic powers over this present darkness, against the spiritual forces of evil in the heavenly places.

EPHESIANS 6:12 ESV

We don't wrestle against flesh and blood. Stop to think about that for a moment. You know what it's like to physically wrestle with someone. No doubt you've had a wrestling match or two with your siblings or friends. But when it comes to the spiritual, our wrestling takes place somewhere else altogether—in the heavenly realms.

For a spiritual battle, we need spiritual weapons. The Bible lists the pieces of God's armor in Ephesians 6: the belt of truth, the breastplate of righteousness, the shoes of peace, the shield of faith, the helmet of salvation, and the sword of the Spirit.

You can "dress" yourself every day in these pieces of armor. Just pray (perhaps as you're putting on your real clothes) that God would clothe you with His protection as well.

The armor of God. . .you don't want to be without it!

God, clothe me in Your full armor today, I pray. Amen.

Breastplate to Guard My Heart

Keep vigilant watch over your heart; that's where life starts.
Don't talk out of both sides of your mouth; avoid careless banter,
white lies, and gossip. Keep your eyes straight ahead; ignore all
sideshow distractions. Watch your step, and the road will stretch out
smooth before you. Look neither right nor left; leave evil in the dust.

Proverbs 4:23–27 MSG

Imagine a police officer headed out to patrol without his bulletproof vest. He wouldn't stand a chance if someone took a shot at him, would he? Now picture a warrior on the battle field. He decides at the last minute that his shield is too heavy so he drops it. . .just as the enemy shoots an arrow his way.

Here's the truth: we need protection. And that spiritual breastplate is the guard you place over your heart. It's not something physical you strap on, like a bulletproof vest, but it's something spiritual you put on each morning when you ask God to guard your heart from any arrows that might be flung your way.

Words hurt. They can leave a scar. And you've been stung by many over the years. But with that breastplate firmly in place, you don't have to be mortally wounded. In fact, those arrows will bounce right off, in Jesus' name!

Lord, thank You for guarding my heart.
Keep it safe, I pray. Amen.

The Sword of the Spirit

*Take the helmet of salvation and the sword
of the Spirit, which is the word of God.*
EPHESIANS 6:17 NIV

Ephesians 6 mentions several pieces of spiritual armor, but perhaps one of the most powerful is the offensive weapon, the sword of the Spirit, which is the Word of God.

So what is the Word of God exactly? It's the Bible, through and through. Cover to cover. The words inside that book are meant to be used as weapons. In fact, you can keep God's Word in your heart so it's there when you need it. Might sound corny, but it's true. All of those scriptures you're working so hard to memorize? They're going to come in very handy when you're in a crisis. You won't even have to plan for it. . .a Bible verse will just come flying out!

So memorize as much as you can. Read as much as you can. Write down verses and put them up on your mirror so you're faced with them as you get ready for your day. And above all, pray that the Lord will take that Word and penetrate your heart with it so it's ready at a moment's notice.

Lord, I will hide Your Word in my heart that I might not sin against You. I will use that Word as a weapon against my enemy. And I will win this battle because the Word is always triumphant against its foes! Amen.

Shoes of Peace

Dear brothers and sisters, I close my letter with these last words:
Be joyful. Grow to maturity. Encourage each other. Live in harmony
and peace. Then the God of love and peace will be with you.
2 CORINTHIANS 13:11 NLT

We all need peace—in our hearts, in our minds, in our speech. Can you imagine how different the world would be if we were all ruled by peace? It would change everything!

Today, take some time to pray for peace on earth. And like the old song says, "Let it begin with me." Ask God to start with your heart, bringing peace in place of turmoil. Then ask Him to bring peace to your family. And to your friendships. And in your schooling situation. And at church. And in your community.

Pray for racial tensions to cease, for peace to take control of the hearts of any wicked people who might be scheming to hurt others, and for our government to be ruled by peace as well.

Let there be peace on earth. It's more than just a saying. It's truly possible, if all of God's people will pray.

Lord, let there be peace on earth, and let it begin with me! Amen.

The Shield of Faith

He replied, "Because you have so little faith. Truly I tell you, if you have faith as small as a mustard seed, you can say to this mountain, 'Move from here to there,' and it will move. Nothing will be impossible for you."
MATTHEW 17:20 NIV

Imagine you had no faith at all. None. Zero. Try to picture it—without faith, you would have no hope. Without hope. . .how would you survive?

God has given you faith as a weapon of warfare, and He expects you to use it! When things look impossible, pull it out and tell the enemy, "You're not going to bring me down! I have faith to believe for the impossible!"

That's what faith is, after all, the ability to go on believing even when common sense says, "Why bother?" It's that added "oomph" that gives you courage to keep going against all odds. It's a belief in what you can't yet see because you feel sure you will one day see it.

Faith is critical to your survival. And it doesn't take much. Just a teensy-tiny bit, in fact. . .the size of a mustard seed (which is about the size of a pinpoint). Just that much and you can move mountains, girl!

I'm a mountain-mover, Lord!

The Helmet of Salvation

*It wasn't so long ago that we ourselves were stupid and stubborn,
easy marks for sin, ordered every which way by our glands, going around
with a chip on our shoulder, hated and hating back. But when God, our kind
and loving Savior God, stepped in, he saved us from all that. It was all his
doing; we had nothing to do with it. He gave us a good bath, and we came
out of it new people, washed inside and out by the Holy Spirit.*

TITUS 3:3–5 MSG

We used to be stupid and stubborn. Now we're saved from all that. When
we come to Christ, when we give Him every area of our lives, He doesn't just
save us from sin; He saves us from our own foolishness, stubbornness, and
selfishness. When we're saved by the sacrifice of Jesus on the cross, we are
made new. Our relationship with God is restored—fully, totally. And our prayer
life comes alive, because the One who saved us is the same One who meets
with us every day.

Have you given your heart to Him? Have you received the gift of salvation?
If not, today is the perfect day!

*Lord, I give myself to You, today. Forgive, cleanse,
and give me new life, I pray. Amen.*

Date:

DEAR GOD, _____
_____
_____
_____

I'm thankful for. . . _____
_____
_____
_____
_____
_____
_____
_____

My worries. . . _____
_____
_____
_____
_____
_____
_____

People I am praying for. . . _____
_____
_____
_____
_____
_____

Here's what's going on in my life. . .

MY NEEDS. . .

Other stuff I need to share with You, God. . .

AMEN.
Thank You, Father,
for hearing my prayers.

WEEK 28

Your Presence, My Joy

You make known to me the path of life; in your presence there is fullness of joy; at your right hand are pleasures forevermore.
PSALM 16:11 ESV

Have you ever over-filled a glass with your favorite beverage? When you do that, it runs down the side and gets all over everything—your hands, the counter, and maybe even your expensive cell phone.

"Overflowing" might not be good when you're talking about soda or milk, but when it comes to your prayer time, God wants it to be overflowing. He wants you to want to be with Him, to desire His presence, to long for your time together in much the same way you long to hang out with your best friend or that boy you have a crush on.

Do you long for God? Does your heart beat with anticipation as you think about spending time in His Word? If not, then perhaps this would be a good day to recommit yourself to Him. He wants an honest, sincere heart, truly, deeply in love with Him. And He wants your prayer time to be not an obligation or a ritual, but a genuine conversation—friend to friend, Father to daughter.

Lord, today I give myself to You. I draw close to You and ask to be refilled to overflowing, Father! Amen.

Everyday Conversations

"When you pray, do not say the same thing over and over again
making long prayers like the people who do not know God.
They think they are heard because their prayers are long."
MATTHEW 6:7 NLV

People make prayer out to be such a stiff, awkward thing, but it's really not. You don't need a special time of day or even a specific way to pray. You just need to be yourself.

Think about it this way: When you sit down to have a chat with a good friend you don't rehearse ahead of time. You don't try to get your words perfect. In fact, you don't even think about that part. You just talk. Normally. Naturally. Comfortably. You speak, you listen. He speaks, he listens. Back and forth you go in easy conversation.

It's the same when you're talking to God. You don't need any big words. You don't need any rehearsed speeches. He simply wants to talk to you, His daughter, the same way you'd chat with your mom at the dinner table. Nothing fancy. Nothing contrived. Nothing formal. Just you. . .being you. And Him. . . being Him.

Lord, I'm so glad my prayer time with You can
be comfortable. Thanks for chatting! Amen.

A Lifestyle of Prayer / Devoted to You

"If you abide in me, and my words abide in you,
ask whatever you wish, and it will be done for you."
JOHN 15:7 ESV

What does it mean to have a lifestyle of prayer? Does it mean you put on a prayer shawl and hide away in your closet for several hours a day? Does it mean you make a huge deal out of separating yourself from others to pray?

No, having a lifestyle of prayer simply means that it's "intrinsic" to you, that it comes naturally. Prayer should be an automatic response to a hard situation. Example: You witness a car accident on the side of the road. You call 9-1-1 and render aid as you're able. Then when the paramedics arrive, what do you do? If prayer comes naturally to you, you automatically begin to pray. No, you don't stand there and make a big scene. But in your heart, the prayer is flowing. And it's happening because you care very much about God's intervention in the situation.

He loves to intervene, you know. And He wants you to remember, with every situation you might face, that He's right there, ready to activate your faith.

Lord, I want prayer to come naturally to me.
May my first call always be to You! Amen.

In the Name of Jesus

*"When the time comes that you see Me again, you will ask Me
no question. For sure, I tell you, My Father will give you whatever
you ask in My name. Until now you have not asked for anything in
My name. Ask and you will receive. Then your joy will be full."*

JOHN 16:23–24 NLV

Why do you suppose we add the words "In Jesus' name" at the end of our prayers? Are we tagging Him on as an afterthought, kind of like you'd tag someone on social media? Or is there more to this idea of praying in His name?

Jesus Himself told His disciples that whatever they asked in His name they would receive. But He wasn't just referring to tossing His name into the prayer as an afterthought. Think about it this way: Before Jesus came to this earth, the disciples simply prayed as they always had. But now that He was leaving them—going back to heaven—He wanted them to be reminded with every single prayer why He had come, for them. He wanted them to remember that His appearance on planet Earth changed absolutely everything.

He came for you too. So pray in His name. Believe in His name. Hope in His name.

*Father, I come to You today in the Name of Your Son, Jesus.
What a powerful Name it is! Amen.*

Prayer Changes Everything

*"Call to me and I will answer you, and will tell you
great and hidden things that you have not known."*
JEREMIAH 33:3 ESV

Prayer changes everything. It can take a horrible day and turn it around completely. It can take a broken relationship and bring peace. It can take a sick body (or mind) and bring healing and comfort. It can cover a grieving heart with holy ointment, and set an emotional roller-coaster ride on the straight and narrow.

Getting from point A to point B is totally up to you though. You have to be the one to stop and pray. Right here. Right now. Without giving excuses or waiting until the time feels right. In the very middle of your problem, you can begin the process of turning things around by simply saying, "Okay, Lord. . .I give up! I can't handle this, but I know You can."

He can, and He will. But only when you're ready to give it to Him, once and for all.

*I won't wait, Lord! I'll be quick to pray. Today I take
my hands off these situations and give them wholly
and completely to You! Bring healing, I pray. Amen.*

Me, a Girl of Prayer!

The first thing I want you to do is pray. Pray every way you know how,
for everyone you know. Pray especially for rulers and their governments
to rule well so we can be quietly about our business of living simply,
in humble contemplation. This is the way our Savior God wants us to live.

1 TIMOTHY 2:1–3 MSG

There are a lot of "callings" on your life, whether you recognize them yet or not. You'll figure out what they are as you get older. But for sure, one calling trumps the rest. You are a girl of prayer. You are called to pray—for your loved ones, yourself, and people across the globe. You might feel limited in what you can do. (Hey, let's face it. . .some of the problems going on out there are way beyond us!) But you can always pray. It's your way to contribute, to do something productive.

When in doubt, pray.

When in distress, pray.

When you're confused, pray.

When you're hurting, pray.

Always. Every time. Without fail.

Pray.

I'm called to be a prayer warrior, Lord. I won't stop. When I feel
there's nothing else I can do, I can always come to You. Amen.

Scripture Index

OLD TESTAMENT

MORE INSPIRATION FOR YOUR HEART!

YOU MATTER

This delightful devotional, created just for teen girls like you, is a beautiful reminder of your purpose. . .your worth. . .your place in the world. One hundred eighty encouraging readings and inspiring prayers, rooted in biblical truth, will reassure your doubting heart. In each devotional reading, you will encounter the bountiful love and grace of your Creator, while coming to understand His plan—for you and you alone.

Flexible Casebound / 978-1-64352-520-4 / $12.99